Your
Hidden
Genius

Your Hidden Genius

The Science-Backed Strategy to Uncovering and Harnessing Your Innate Talents

BETSY WILLS AND ALEX ELLISON

HARVEST

An Imprint of WILLIAM MORROW

HarperCollins books may be purchased for educational, business, or
sales promotional use. For information, please email the Special Markets
Department at SPsales@harpercollins.com.

FIRST EDITION

Designed by Chloe Foster

Illustrations © 2024 Annatto LLC. AnnattoCreates.com.

Library of Congress Cataloging-in-Publication Data has been applied for.

ISBN 978-0-06-328987-1

24 25 26 27 28 LBC 5 4 3 2 1

To Anna Ball

Contents

Introduction

A Lofty Bump of Humor

In 1873, thirty-eight-year-old Samuel Clemens was hitting his stride, building his reputation as a humorist, a writer, and a public skeptic. That year, he released his only co-written novel—*The Gilded Age*—a biting satirical critique of greed and political corruption. It had been just ten years since he'd adopted his pen name, Mark Twain; a year since the birth of his first daughter, Susy; and mere months since he'd received a patent for a self-pasting scrapbook.

Around this time, Twain felt a nagging question weighing on him. Perhaps in spite of—or because of—his growing success and self-actualization, he wanted to know whether there was some way for a person to objectively assess his "temperament" or most innate traits and qualities. He wondered: *Could a person's character be read like a chart of the constellations?*

To find out, Twain made an appointment with the leading phrenologist of the day, Lorenzo Niles Fowler. (He didn't identify himself as Mark Twain, but used an altogether different alias.) Phrenologists in the late nineteenth century claimed to be able to describe a person's character and personality by simply "reading" the bumps and cavities on a person's skull, much like one would read a topographic map.[1] And so, the curious but always skeptical Twain walked into Fowler's London office, with the request that his own head be mapped. The initial read was quite complimentary, recalled Twain. After much poking and prodding of Twain's cranium, the phrenologist "said I possessed amazing courage, an abnormal spirit of daring, a pluck, a stern will, a fearlessness that were without limit." These qualities were ascertained by the size of the bumps on Twain's head.

"But then he foraged over on the other side of my skull," noted Twain, "and found a hump there which he called 'caution.' This hump was so tall, so mountainous, that it reduced my courage-bump to a mere hillock by comparison." If not for this "Matterhorn of caution," he said, "I would have been one of the bravest men that ever lived." But the real doubt arose when Fowler fingered the part of his skull where a slight cavity appeared. "He startled me by saying that that cavity represented the total absence of the sense of humor!"

Had Twain really lacked a sense of humor, he would not have found this funny, and would not, therefore, have chosen to go back a second time to Fowler's London office. This time, he presented himself as the famous author Mark Twain. And during this visit, to the author's great delight, Fowler discovered "the loftiest bump of humor he had ever encountered in his lifelong experience!"[2]

While Twain made fun of the pseudoscience, he was still left without an answer to his question about reading a person's character, and the answer would not appear within his lifetime.

We laugh at phrenology today. But there's no denying the persistent human urge to know ourselves—and our possibilities—as well as we can. We so desperately want to know what is in our nature, and about the gifts with which we've been endowed, that we will look anywhere, turn to anyone, and pay any price, especially when it comes to discerning how we want to share those gifts with the world. And nowhere is that urge more compelling than when it comes to choosing our life's work.

The Changing Workplace

Landing on the right career seems more important today than ever before; in recent decades, work has eclipsed family, community, and religion as our primary source of meaning and identity. In a shift accelerated by the Covid-19 pandemic in 2020, technological advances have largely erased the boundary between our personal and professional lives. Right or wrong, we have become our work, and our work has become us. But when your personal sense of identity, self-esteem, and mental health are so deeply tied to what you do, what happens if you don't actually like your work? Or worse, what if you lose your job?

Like millions of others, you may have recently decided that spending the vast majority of your waking hours doing work you don't particularly care about is no longer worth it. In 2021, during what came to be called the "Great Resignation," a record 47.4 million American workers left their jobs.[3] Those who stayed were more disengaged than in prior decades. In 2022, the Gallup organization, which tracks employee engagement year after year, reported that a mere 21 percent of employees felt motivated at work, and more people than ever before were experiencing high levels of stress. "Living for the weekend" and "work is just a paycheck" became mantras. As Gallup observed, "Most respondents said that they don't find their work meaningful, don't think their lives are going well or don't feel hopeful about their future."[4]

Even before the Covid-19 pandemic, the nature of work was changing at a breathtaking pace. But when Covid struck, the world turned upside down. Hundreds of thousands of businesses shut down in a matter of months, and millions suddenly found themselves without a paycheck.[5] Those who could least afford it were the hardest hit: Of the 9.6 million jobs lost in 2020, the overwhelming majority of those positions employed people in the bottom quarter of wage distribution.[6] In the first thirteen months of the pandemic, eight million workers were laid off and the restaurant industry hemorrhaged $280 billion in sales.[7] Under pressure to care for children and family members, a stunning 3.5 million working mothers left the workforce, and even today over a million fewer mothers are holding down jobs than in 2019.[8]

The pandemic also triggered a massive shift in *how* we work. By October 2020, 70 percent of employed Americans were performing their jobs from home all or most of the time, and increasing numbers found they enjoyed greater work flexibility.[9]

For some, working remotely is burning us out faster than commuting ever did. For thirty-five-year-old Nikita Ovtchinikov, traveling several times a month for in-person meetings was an integral part of his work as a Silicon Valley enterprise sales executive. He might, for example, find himself scheduled for a meeting in Los Angeles and having "to fly down there from San Francisco, maybe cancel some of the calls due to the travel time, have lunch with colleagues, and fly home." But when the pandemic hit, all of his meetings became remote, and their frequency increased threefold. "It was bananas," Ovtchinikov says, "both draining and exhausting." He realized the travel that once seemed like such a nuisance was actually a much-needed cushion in a hectic and unrelenting workday. Even if remote work can lead to higher productivity in some cases, he noted, "it comes with a cost." Human beings aren't cut out for such rapid attention-switching.[10]

Still, not having to commute to work retains its appeal for many. In 2021, 80 percent of Americans working from home said they didn't want to return to the office full-time, while a whopping 95 percent of workers were considering changing jobs.[11] Americans today are realizing they will be working at many more kinds of jobs, and for many more years, than previous generations. Combined with longer life expectancies and more working years, the average twelve jobs held by baby boomers over the course of their careers is set to rise with subsequent generations.[12]

Meanwhile, employees no longer seem content to work grueling hours, perhaps as an investment in their future earnings or title, without a more immediate payoff. The phrase "quiet quitting" generated millions of views on TikTok, as many young professionals rejected the notion of working longer and longer hours to prove themselves worthy of promotion. According to the *Wall Street Journal*, these employees didn't want to leave work altogether, but they yearned to spend more time outside the office doing things that interested them, such as being with their families or enjoying sports and hobbies.[13] It's not just Gen Z and young millennials either. Millions of older workers, too, resent spending their days watching the clock tick. As many have told us, "I can't wait until I retire so that I can have time to work on my _____ [fill in the blank: art, music, volunteer work, family, et cetera]."

Of course, every job involves some amount of plodding through familiar drills. And certainly, there are distinct changes in the way we work—and a broader movement toward more diverse and inclusive workplaces—that are influencing these employment trends. But the vast dissatisfaction we currently face goes deeper. It's about the rampant, fundamental mismatch between our natural abilities and the jobs we routinely perform. Like a decoupled chain, this disconnect weakens our staying power and makes it harder to find satisfaction at work. It amplifies the weight of anxiety, boredom, overwork, demands to re-skill, frustration with management, low pay, lack of benefits, poor working conditions, and any number of other factors, driving employees of every rank to simply check out.[14]

The good news is that all of this frustration and unrealized potential is entirely preventable, and the solution isn't just about complying with a shrug or finding a different job where you may be equally stalled. The answer lies in switching tactics. It's about harnessing modern insights and technologies (far advanced from the quackery of Mark Twain's era) to assess whether your work life and avocations are in harmony with your authentic self. By discovering your hidden genius—the complete tapestry of your personality, interests, and, most important, your aptitudes—you have the means to unlock your potential. With the help of this book, you can begin to understand your own natural talents and what they can tell you about your life, career, and relationships. And we promise, no head thumping required.

Starved for Guidance

When it comes to choosing our most satisfying work lives, we face many challenges. Despite the strides we've made in science, data aggregation, and technology since the late 1800s, most people today default to guesswork or rely on incomplete information about potential careers. Young people have always felt pressured by loved ones, circumstances, or immediate needs to "settle" for work that may or may not suit them. Or they don't have models in their family, friends, and personal networks to realize the incredible breadth of their employment options. With no concrete or objective guidance, they are apt to lean heavily on the opinions of their peers and other well-meaning people around them. Lacking a complete understanding of what kinds of work might best fit their skills, they end up relying largely on assumptions and stereotypes.

Thus, steeped in unconscious gender roles, a majority of high school boys still tend to be interested in "masculine" jobs such as engineering or construction, while girls veer toward work traditionally performed by women, such as teaching or nursing.[15] A recent study on career choices and gender disparity revealed how classic gender roles permeate our personal aspirations. When free to follow their career passions, female study participants gravitated toward primary caregiver roles, while the men sought to become the breadwinners. Following our passions might seem like the best way to express our true selves. But as it turns out, this freedom can instead lead us to fall back on social norms that feel safe and predictable.[16] As the Scottish psychiatrist R. D. Laing observed, "We learn to be who we are told we are."[17]

But what's the alternative?

Unwinding the Thread

We do, in fact, have a choice: we can follow our enduring traits like a guiding thread through our lives. Writers, actors, and directors who tell stories for a living rely on the notion of an imaginary thread that weaves through a narrative. They call this the "through line." It is the underlying motive of characters, the hidden force that drives their behavior. The events surrounding the protagonist may change, but his or her basic through line remains consistent and ever present throughout the story. Your hidden genius is this essential thread. It contributes to your individuality. It comprises the enduring and distinctive aspects of what makes you, you. Your aptitudes, along with your interests and personality, are the raw materials—the fuel that propels your life.

Discovering your hidden genius is a gradual process. Your starting point—discovered through the assessment you'll begin in Chapter 3—will help you to uncover your own unique combination of aptitudes, interests, and personality traits. Once you apply the results of this assessment to your career, they will help you to find the work and other pursuits that can most fulfill and satisfy you. You will be able to apply your newfound self-awareness not just in choosing your career, but also in navigating other aspects of your life.

How We Discovered Our Own Hidden Genius

BETSY'S STORY

On a warm spring morning, as I stood looking at my reflection in the bathroom mirror, I came to a sudden, painful realization. I was thirty-three years old, and I was nowhere close to fulfilling my potential.

Having married ten years earlier, I had filled a lot of socially prescribed roles. I'd tackled college, gotten married, worked a couple of great jobs, and brought two children into the world. I had also become heavily involved in my community. From the outside, my life probably looked perfect. I had everything in the world I could want or need: healthy children, a happy marriage, a lovely home, and good friends. But on the inside, I felt antsy. I had no reason to think of myself as unhappy, but at that moment, I suddenly understood that I was living my life much like a car passenger on a very pleasant trip. I just wasn't driving.

So the realization hit: I'd lost track of my own life. Time suddenly mattered. I knew that if I followed my family's genetic map, I might be lucky enough to live to be a hundred. What would I do with my future life? I hadn't truly considered how I might contribute to the world more broadly, beyond my own home, or how I could enrich myself through learning over the decades to come. I decided it was time to determine my own life course.

A respected friend encouraged me to seek advice from the esteemed Johnson O'Connor Research Foundation. At the assessment center in Atlanta (which they call the "human engineering laboratory"), I spent two days answering surveys on my personality and interests and also performing timed exercises designed to uncover my individual aptitudes. Afterward, a counselor walked through my results with me. As I listened to her describe me in sometimes disturbing detail, I felt as if someone had suddenly turned the lights on. She pointed me to areas of personal potential that I hadn't fully understood, highlighting aspects of myself I had discounted or ignored. The counselor helped me see that I had spent years unconsciously inserting myself into other people's categorical boxes.

Armed with my assessment results, I came to understand my quirks and talents within a context and a language that made sense. I felt inspired and motivated. Even better, I saw how I might apply them to my own future. I enrolled in a graduate program for Human and Organization Development, and from there I got a job as a marketing and investor relations manager in the financial services industry. My boss there was interested in the opportunities that technology offered for transforming education and career services. Together, we made the online aptitude assessment company YouScience a reality. (To top it off, I also started a blog about contemporary art, which I found to be an extraordinarily fulfilling hobby.)

ALEX'S STORY

Growing up, I never doubted my abilities for a moment; I just never had a clue what they were. Dreaming big, feeling the world stretch out before me, I believed myself capable of just about anything. No fantasy was too taxing for my young imagination. What I lacked in self-awareness, I made up for in gusto and blind determination.

After graduating from college in 2010, I took a job leading a freshman honors seminar on community engagement at the University of Nevada in Reno. The more I worked to connect students to opportunities, the more I found myself longing to help all incoming college freshmen approach their education with more clarity and intentionality. I also wanted to help them avoid incurring heavy student debt. To do that, I realized I'd need to start working with high school kids.

In 2013, I launched my own consultancy as a college and career counselor. My job is to introduce young adults to their true natural aptitudes, to help them explore opportunities to exercise those talents, and to point them in a general direction that may or may not include a college degree. I hope to save them wasted time, energy, and dollars, and steer them toward occupations that will bring them joy and success.

In reality, most of us approach this task from an impossible position, with only a vague idea of our true strengths and where they might prove most useful. But how can we be expected to assemble the jigsaw puzzle of our lives with the lights off? Forced to feel our way around in the dark, we can only guess at the picture we are creating and what it might mean. Just imagine what we might do with the lights on. For instance, I always wondered why I felt so fatigued by brainstorming sessions, group work, and "decision-by-committee" situations. I thought there was something wrong with me. In meetings, I'd get fidgety whenever someone said something like "Let's go back to the drawing board," or "Have we considered all the other alternatives?" I'd find myself staring at the clock, my attention and energy draining away into my seat.

When I took an aptitude assessment in 2014, I learned that my inborn talents were closely aligned with many jobs involving writing, such as journalism. This discovery was an invitation to get back to something I had loved doing as a child, allowing me to pinpoint a part of what had been missing from my life. But aside from writing, my most pronounced strength lies in my ability to be both highly focused and good at implementation. While I don't always have the quickest response or the most ideas, I am usually the one to move a stagnant group along, and I have a knack for identifying the most promising ideas. I use this aptitude to cheerlead those who feel uninspired to take their first step into something or to help those clouded by indecision to find a path forward.

Today, my job is about giving young adults permission to get to know themselves better, so that they can navigate their lives with confidence.

And while I didn't know it before, the assessment revealed that guidance counseling sits right at the intersection of my aptitudes, values, and interests. I've since learned that aptitude awareness is a nonbiased, no-BS way to show that the best way to navigate our careers—and lives—is to uncover our hidden genius.

So, What Is an Aptitude?

Aptitudes are your own unique, inborn talents, the foundation from which you can develop skills. They are the underlying components of who you are that common personality and interest assessments cannot discern. Most important, aptitudes are your most reliably enduring features.

While many people lump the domains of aptitudes, interests, and personality together and speak of them interchangeably, in fact, they are distinctly different from one another. Frequently confused with skills or abilities, aptitudes play a critical role in career satisfaction. They are also the first and most important focus of this book.

Researchers have identified dozens of measurable aptitudes, everything from perfect pitch to a facility for foreign languages to the ability to withstand staring into very bright light. Some aptitudes are physical, like finger dexterity or hand grip; others are cognitive, like the ability to imagine what a two-dimensional diagram would look like in three dimensions. Some, such as the ability to hear a random noise and immediately identify its corresponding musical note, are so rare that only a lucky few are endowed with them.

Aptitudes don't develop by themselves. To blossom into something truly special, hard work and practice are required. Knowing your aptitudes can motivate you to set goals that you might never have imagined. For example, consider Michael Phelps. The six foot four Olympian was born with what some experts call the perfect body for swimming. His powerful legs are the same length as someone four inches shorter, so he can propel himself through the water with less drag to slow him down. Yet he also has the torso length of a man four inches taller, giving him extra-long arms and a greater reach in a sport where races can be won by a mere fraction of an inch.[18] This is Phelps's raw material—the equivalent of his basic aptitudes. But those gifts alone wouldn't have been enough to transform him into a champion swimmer. To end up with twenty-eight Olympic medals—still the most won by any athlete in history—Phelps had to put in years of training and practice.

Complex and multifaceted, aptitudes can only be gauged using objective psychometric assessments. These measures are designed with a high standard of scientific rigor rooted in many different fields, including developmental psychology, biological psychology, industrial-organizational psychology (the study of human behavior in organizations and the workplace), neuroscience, behavioral genetics, and psychometrics. In general, today's aptitude assessments are analogous to MRI machines; they can see beneath the surface to reveal conditions and qualities (or traits) we may not know we have. Even better, this information is based on objective measures of performance: Can you spot the pattern in this set of numbers? Can you distinguish this slightly lighter shade of blue from that slightly darker shade of blue? Can you arrange these sentences in a logical order?

Until recently, aptitude assessment was a one-on-one activity, delivered to a client by a trained counselor over many hours at a specialized testing center. At an average cost of $750, plus transportation and the two days it took to complete a full evaluation, these tests are out of reach for most of the population. But in the past decade, technology has revolutionized this formerly bespoke service, allowing it to be digitized and democratized. The price of aptitude testing has now fallen by orders of magnitude, making it accessible to more and more people from all walks of life.

Career guidance professionals have long recognized the critical importance of aptitudes in finding happiness and fulfillment at work. This book is about how we unlock that knowledge and leverage it for maximum impact. For over a century, aptitudes have been the focus of research and specialized use, yet they have lingered in relative obscurity. It's time for us to recognize and embrace this foundational part of ourselves, because doing so can literally change our lives.

Take Rebecca, for example. She used to stubbornly point to a couple of Cs in math as proof that she was not a "math kid." But once she took her aptitude assessment, she realized how wrong she had been. "Sprinkled throughout my life, there were actually signs that I am not only good with numbers, but I enjoy working with them too. After all, I was the junior class treasurer!" Recognizing this hidden talent prompted Rebecca to pursue higher-level math courses in college that she would have normally shied away from. She even took an interest in data science, later applying it to an exciting career as director of marketing for a small digital agency that serves mental health and addiction treatment centers. She turned out to be a math kid after all. But like so many of us, she only made this discovery as an adult.[19] It's easy to point to poor grades as evidence of our weak points; however, conventional school and assessment measures overlook some of our most important aptitudes. At the time, Rebecca had no way of knowing that she indeed had a hidden facility with numbers; in her case, lower grades in math spoke more to her negative classroom experiences than to any deficiency in Numerical Reasoning.

Discovering your aptitudes with the help of an accessible, modern assessment tool is meant to offer guidance of this kind sooner, rather than later. It is not intended as a pigeonholing mechanism that makes people pursue careers they don't want, forcing them to give up their dreams. On the contrary, aptitude assessment can help us to recognize options or alternatives we never knew we had. It lays the groundwork for success by pointing us toward vocations inherently suited to our natural talents and jobs that are in demand. Any given set of aptitudes represents opportunities in multiple industries.

Equally important, aptitude assessment can help us narrow down a mind-boggling multitude of possible careers. The optimistic and largely unfeasible American credo of "You can do anything!" leads to an overwhelming and oppressive tyranny of choice; one that paralyzes college students and midlife career switchers, alike. But the enormity of this choice is an illusion. With effort and practice we can, indeed, do many things. But that doesn't mean we always should. If the work you are doing doesn't allow you to flourish you can easily get stuck pouring all your effort into something without any lasting payoff. In the worst cases, you can find yourself pushing harder and harder toward some goal, yet achieving less and less.

As we bob and weave through a changing career landscape, we have new opportunities to maximize our skills, find jobs that reflect our personal values, and destabilize lasting work stereotypes around gender, socioeconomics, and race. And discovering who you are and what you have to offer the world using rigorous scientific aptitude assessment can help offset the biases of many other tests. For example, Western intelligence measures such as the IQ test are known to emphasize the ideas and values of their creators, to the detriment of test takers with non-Western cultural frames of reference, and college entrance exams tend to favor those who can afford to pay expensive coaches and tutors.[20] But trying to study for an aptitude assessment is futile; it would only skew the results. Moreover, the measure of aptitudes such as the ability to recognize number patterns can be quantified impartially, because such skills transcend language and culture.

Using aptitude assessments for educational and occupational guidance can reduce workplace bias by capturing a more diverse talent pool that includes varied genders, races, and economic backgrounds. More important, the results of these assessments force us to reconsider our own internal assumptions about our potential to achieve, paving the way for more girls to explore stereotypically male fields and vice versa.[21] Input from social media, entertainment outlets, and well-intentioned parents, teachers, coaches, and friends often reinforces traditional gender roles and highlights familiar career paths.[22] After all, it's hard to be interested in a career you've never heard of. But what if we could match our skills and interests, like puzzle pieces, against all possible careers and learn where we would fit with absolute certainty?

Given the ever-evolving workplace, constantly changing skill requirements, and a vast swath of employees suddenly wanting more fulfilling work, knowing our aptitudes is vital. Such knowledge enables us to have greater confidence, to be the entrepreneurs of our own careers, to make smarter choices, and to optimize our talents. More than that, knowing our aptitudes helps us live a satisfying life.

Three Distinct Contributors

If your hidden genius were an actual rope, it would be a braided one with three strands. The most critical and previously elusive of these is your aptitude profile. But your interests and personality also play a key role in shaping your career potential. Indeed, for many years, career counselors relied entirely on interest and personality assessments. Without attending to aptitudes, however, this narrow focus led to far too many (albeit unintentional) career shipwrecks. The true power of interests and personality measures can only be realized when joined with and interpreted alongside aptitudes.

Interests are your preferences. They motivate you to improve and hone your abilities based on what you think you love to do, allowing you to train, gain greater expertise, and become more successful at whatever you choose. But interests are fickle; they can change over time, depending on your situation, environment, age, or your individual personality traits.

Take Emma Lock, for example. In an interview with *WorkLife*'s Adam Grant, Lock discussed how her childhood dream of becoming "a flamingo" morphed into veterinary aspirations. But the realities of work as a veterinarian, including "dealing with tendons and putting thermometers in animals' rectums," soon made her realize "it's not really my thing."

Next, Lock took her love of animals into zookeeper training, a job that ultimately triggered a severe hay allergy that made it difficult to breathe at work. "But because I loved the animals so much, I stayed," she noted. After years of suffering, she stepped back and realized that the part of her job she loved the most—teaching visitors about the animals—only comprised a small portion of her time. She finally acknowledged that zookeeping "wasn't the job that was best suited to me, given my personality and my talents" (not to mention her allergies).[23] Today she works as a public speaker and online animal educator known as "Emzotic," embracing her true calling to teach others the most fun, exciting, and unexpected tidbits about animals.

Our interests can draw us deeply and consistently into a given topic, but only for as long as our fascination lasts. The more experience Lock gained, the more she learned about her underlying aptitudes and the type of work that would bring her sustained fulfillment, not just satisfy her interests. This key distinction has caught the eye of some of the nation's top graduate schools, including Harvard Law School, whose admissions department now places particular emphasis on life experience in selecting their best applicants. Whereas the entering classes of two decades ago were largely recent college graduates, a vast majority of today's first-year law students at Harvard have had at least one full year of work experience.[24]

Grasping the difference between the fascination or fantasy of a job and its everyday reality can help us seek out the most suitable work experiences and find the most fulfilling careers. Still, interests remain a relatively fast and easy indicator of what we might want to do with our lives. For assessing interests, career practitioners have long used reliable instruments such as the Strong Interest Inventory. Aligned with the theories of American psychologist John Holland, these subjective questionnaires can be self-scored and administered cheaply, efficiently, and at scale. Successfully used for more than eighty-five years, they have become widely accepted as a standard among career guidance professionals.

The problem with interest surveys is that when used as a stand-alone instrument (as they have been in most high schools and colleges since the 1950s), their accuracy becomes less reliable. Used in isolation, they become information boomerangs that bring back little more than a repackaged version of what we put into them. Instead of offering new insights, their results can easily point you toward a future that already seems self-evident (such as what your parents always told you to do) or jobs and industries with which you're familiar (such as the careers featured at school career days), regardless of what type of work might be the best fit for you. The results are not terribly surprising; after all, it's hard to express preferences for things you've never seen or tried. But in a world of glutted industries and fierce job competition, the overemphasis on interests has real and troubling consequences. In the mid-2000s, for example, culinary school enrollment increased with the popularity of reality TV shows about cooking.[25] Likewise, interest in criminal justice soared in proportion to the ratings of the American crime drama *CSI: Crime Scene Investigation*, even as the growth rate for police detective and criminal investigator jobs has lagged behind the national average.[26]

When used without factoring in personality and aptitudes, survey-based tools can also perpetuate learned assumptions and conscious or unconscious stereotypes. The resulting misguidance can do systematic harm to members of a broad swath of groups, including people of color, women, and those from economically challenged communities. For example, one 2020 University of Missouri study highlighted these negative effects on school-age girls. The researchers found that, when treated as the sole source of career guidance, career-interest surveys can—and do—funnel girls away from high-paying, high-growth fields and toward less lucrative, familiar "female" roles. What is familiar influences our interests, and interests drive our career decisions. Without the opportunity to recognize and understand our own aptitudes and how they complement our interests, our paths tend to converge on the most popular, already congested highways rather than on more personalized, satisfying byways.

Personality is broadly defined in psychology as your characteristic pattern of thinking, feeling, and behaving. Psychologists agree that there are five basic dimensions of personality, commonly referred to as the "Big 5." They are categorized as extroversion, agreeableness, openness, conscientiousness, and neuroticism.[27] Admittedly, these are roomy terms and serve only as a blueprint for understanding the main dimensions of personality, which has an unlimited number of nuances. And within this basic model, people possess varying amounts of the Big 5 qualities and fall along a continuum between the extremes of each.

It is also important to understand that the science of personality traits has different applications. You may have heard of certain popular measures for personality traits, including Myers-Briggs, DiSC, and the Enneagram. Psychologists deploy some of these tools to better understand their patients, while organizational behaviorists utilize them to study team dynamics. Depending on the context, such tools can drive meaningful conversations and serve as valuable conduits for self-discovery.

But while knowing your personality traits can help you identify your motivations and the work settings and roles that suit you best, when it comes to finding the best career fit they are only part of the answer. The trick is to recognize your own personal configuration of aptitudes, interests, and personality, and then honor and nurture them to build a more authentic and fulfilling life.

Moving Ahead

Thanks to innovative advances in technology, the current field of career guidance has taken a huge leap forward. The assessment batteries commonly offered in high school and college now include measures of aptitudes as well as personality and interests. In 2023 alone, YouScience administered more than a million of these aptitude assessments. Entire states such as Georgia have adopted aptitude testing in their high schools, recognizing that our life-altering, expense-laden decisions about our education and careers should not be some random, data-starved activity.

We live in a world where professional categories change constantly and job obsolescence has become the norm. By necessity, our reassessments of our work never stop. And so, whether you are starting your career, rethinking, retooling, reinventing, relaunching, or retiring, it is never too late to discover and embrace your hidden genius.

Following your innate talents also has massive implications for our society as a whole. As more people choose to travel this path, greater numbers will focus on developing their own unique gifts rather than worrying about their perceived deficits. A confidence born of self-knowledge will help us pursue the most urgent work, and together we will mobilize our potential to advance. As our friends, loved ones, and co-workers assess their own aptitudes, their cycles of self-doubt will break. And as the pursuit of self-knowledge spreads, we'll see a rise in the number of people developing skills in critical areas, thanks to their new understanding of how to link their education to desired outcomes.

This book will help you choose vocations for which you are well suited and find the activities in which you are predisposed to excel. It also offers a template for finding deep and fulfilling meaning throughout your life, from your career, hobbies and service to your relationships with family, friends, and your community. The resulting realignment between your natural aptitudes, interests and personality and your work makes the necessary task of reevaluating and changing jobs—and even careers— during our working years a less formidable one. As you navigate an uncertain future, we hope you will find this book to be an essential resource for guiding you toward a path that both satisfies and inspires you.

Part I

A Better Way

There's a thread you follow. It goes among

things that change. But it doesn't change.

People wonder about what you are pursuing.

You have to explain about the thread.

But it is hard for others to see.

While you hold it you can't get lost.

Tragedies happen; people get hurt

or die; and you suffer and get old.

Nothing you do can stop time's unfolding.

You don't ever let go of the thread.

—William Stafford, "The Way It Is"

CHAPTER 1

Welcome to Your Hidden Genius

We must each lead a way of life with self-awareness and compassion, to do as much as we can. Then, whatever happens, we will have no regrets.

—Dalai Lama

"You know sex dice?" Swedish YouTuber Simone Giertz asks as she turns to rifle through a box in her Los Angeles studio. Dressed in grease-stained coveralls, her red hair pulled back in a ponytail, the thirty-three-year-old places three dice on the desk between us. "We've basically created our own," she says; only instead of making X-rated suggestions to spice things up in the bedroom, these dice are designed to spur innovative, wildly imaginative creations. Each of the dice has a theme: one has different materials on each face, another has objects, and a third, properties. So, for example, you might roll them and get "Cardboard," "Vehicle," and "No Circles." You could then play around with different ways to "make a vehicle out of cardboard, only you're not allowed to use any circles." Giertz grins at the thought.

The idea for the dice first came to Laura Kampf, Giertz's friend and dice cocreator, in a dream. When she woke up, Kampf called Giertz to share her exciting new inspiration. What better way to jumpstart an innovative project than to season the options with a bit of chance? So, the idea dice were born.

When Giertz first opened her assessment results during our interview, her excitement was palpable. What traits could possibly be at play in her self-created role as an engineer, inventor, and online comedian? What was her unique combination of aptitudes, personality, and interests? She confessed that she used to dream of being a child prodigy, reveling in the ability to inspire awe in adults. "My entire self-worth was defined by the grades I got. So, if I got a B on a test, it was like, I was a bad human." Looking back, she now realizes that she was aligning herself with others' ideas of success. She figured out the achiever's formula, then mastered it. And, in the process, "I attached my self-worth to it." The tests, presentations, and other academic assessments she excelled at became accolades that she used to define herself. These were also the talents she recognized. In her mind, at least, "high achiever" was her greatest core aptitude.

Giertz had tried myriad successful-sounding jobs, including a prestigious role editing articles about Swedish culture for the Swedish government. "It was flattering," she recalls. "I was the youngest editor they'd ever hired."[1] But in this position, Giertz overtaxed certain aptitudes while underutilizing others. As she later learned, though her mix of prominent aptitudes was diverse, it did not include the keen eye of an editor.

Eventually, Giertz became so sapped by her lifelong pursuit of the perfect job that the only place she was able to find solace was in the messiest, most imperfect work she could imagine. The repeated mistakes, iterations, and tinkering of her online experiments as "the Queen of Shitty Robots" not only relieved her angst, it drew millions of viewers to her YouTube channel. Some of Giertz's most popular videos feature her creating and testing a toothbrushing helmet, a wake-up alarm that slaps you in the face, an automatic vegetable chopper, and various other "useless machines," as she calls them. Other inventions include various household products such as a chair made out of an old satellite dish and a top-of-the-fridge junk organizer. The video that shows her retrofitting a $100,000 Tesla into a small pickup truck by sawing half of it off garnered over 7.5 million views.[2]

When we walked Giertz through her assessment results, her eyes lit up and her whole demeanor changed. Like so many others who view them for the first time, she felt a combination of relief and pride at finally having the right words to describe what she'd always felt. Her results highlighted her ability to quickly generate wild and crazy ideas, visualize entirely original contraptions in three dimensions, and problem-solve in the face of countless unknowns. These traits had been with her all along. But only now did she recognize them as the unique assets that had occasionally, in the wrong settings, felt like deficits. She was much more than an achiever or a child prodigy. She had a set of traits that, when nurtured, allowed her to find a kind of success only Simone Giertz could achieve. And it just so happens that her ideal career path includes inventing a mechanical helmet mounted with hands that shovel popcorn into your mouth.

Your personality, aptitudes, and interests will be revealed through your participation in a series of short, gamelike exercises and brief questionnaires (see Chapter 3). Of course, it would be foolish to suggest that any one assessment could capture all of your many personal nuances and complexities. Ultimately, the configuration and context of your results are more important than any single preference or aptitude you have, because each activity, career, or vocation aligns with specific patterns or profiles. The subtle relationship between these patterns is part of their magic. Even pivoting a few degrees right or left in a particular job can mean the difference between apathy and enthusiasm.

For example, instead of quitting, a dissatisfied lawyer who discovers a strength in visualizing three-dimensional objects might try to find clients who work in construction or engineering. She could shift her practice to focus on patent law, or start taking a weekend ceramics class. The key is to embrace your own particular combination of patterns, and the internal forces they signify, so you can seek out complementary pursuits and meet each new challenge with confidence and enthusiasm.

Your Untapped Reservoir of Potential

We devote the greater part of this book to unpacking aptitudes, in particular, because technology has made information about them more accessible, and because they are less known. They are crucially important for understanding ourselves and our most promising futures.

To understand the term *aptitudes*, it first helps to understand what they are not. Although aptitudes do represent a form of intelligence, and a few correlate with IQ, they are not an intelligence measure. IQ claims to capture a person's overall, objective "intelligence" based on a single battery of questions. But aptitudes are more like a diagram of your brain's inner hardwiring. They are diverse and dynamic. Aptitudes can influence your personality, but they aren't measured through popular questionnaires such as StrengthsFinder, the Enneagram of Personality, or the Myers-Briggs Type Indicator. Aptitudes are not interests, and they're not achievements or skills. More accurately, they are the raw material from which you can develop skills.

Aptitudes are the natural abilities and talents with which we are born; we don't learn them, but we can improve upon them with practice. Fully formed after puberty, our aptitudes are enduring, permanent aspects of who we are—crucial elements that we can call upon and develop over our lifetimes. Everyone has aptitudes to varying degrees, in combinations as unique to each of us as a fingerprint. Most people pursue careers in response to random influences, decisions, and opportunities, so they aren't aware that they have hidden natural talents. They have no clear idea of what their talents are or the array of possibilities they present.

Most of us see the Milky Way as a pale, purplish cloud that stretches across the sky on clear nights when there isn't too much light pollution. But if you ever look at it through a telescope, you can actually see what that glowing haze is: a dizzying multitude of individual stars. You probably already knew that the Milky Way, as seen from Earth, is just a view of our galaxy from the inside. But a telescope turns this knowledge into a tangible, jaw-dropping truth. With a little research, we can start to learn the names and ages of each star, their movements, and their relationships with one another.

Now, imagine we had a tool that could, like a human telescope, zoom in on our own inner points of light. With it, we could begin to understand ourselves and make new discoveries, just as humans have explored our galaxy and the universe beyond. Think of your aptitudes as your inner stars, and the assessment included in this book as your own personal telescope.

Aptitude assessments measure how pronounced each of your aptitudes are; however, whether any one of your aptitudes is weak or strong matters less than how your personal array of traits interact and complement one another. Your results will identify the areas in which you have the most promise based on your deepest inclinations.

Over the past century, psychometricians have developed valid and reliable assessments to measure dozens of aptitudes, ranging from pitch sensitivity and hand-eye coordination to pattern or numbers memory, idea fluency, analytical reasoning, and hue discrimination.

Knowing which specific aptitudes are our most pronounced emboldens us to pursue the activities that hold the greatest promise and come most easily to us. It also allows us to personalize our training and work based on a confident knowledge of what makes us unique. As career coach and Rockport Institute founder Nicholas Lore wrote in his 1998 book *The Pathfinder*, "Everyone is born with a unique group of talents [or aptitudes] that are as individual as a fingerprint or a snowflake. These talents give each person a special ability to do certain kinds of tasks easily and happily, yet also make other tasks seem like pure torture. Talents are completely different from acquired knowledge. Your natural, inherited talents remain with you, unchanging for your entire life."[3]

Still, motivation and effort can trump any of these natural proclivities, and pursuits that engage less dominant aptitudes can still be attained. Practice always breeds improvement, and there is real value in improving abilities for which we have no natural aptitude. Mastering such skills may take more time and commitment than what would be required of someone with strong aptitudes in those areas. But any career involves diverse skills to complete a variety of tasks, some of which are more challenging than others. If you are willing and motivated to put in the effort, whether you have exactly the right aptitudes for a certain type of work can be less important. After all, learning a job is often harder than doing the job; the learning curve to competence can be steep, but once you've scaled it, you'll find yourself on even ground.

Of Aptitudes and Amplifiers

All aptitudes are not created equal. Indeed, a select few have a significant influence on your professional and personal life. Below are descriptions of what we call the Core Four, the essential aptitudes that are foundational to self-awareness. Following the Core Four are descriptions of the two most important Amplifiers, talents that can complement the Core Four and magnify your effectiveness.

The Core Four are:

SPATIAL VISUALIZATION

Spatial Visualization is the ability to look at a two-dimensional figure and visualize what it would look like in three dimensions. This aptitude is a true fork in the road. Either you have it, or you don't. If you do, it is important to recognize this aptitude as an itch that must be scratched. You may pursue a career in architecture, landscape design, engineering, or some other spatially focused job. But if those occupations don't interest you and your job does not make use of Spatial Visualization, consider picking up model-building or ceramics as a hobby. We know one frustrated lawyer who bought broken toasters at garage sales and spent his spare time taking them apart and repairing them, just for fun. While that's not necessarily what we'd suggest for you, you will need an outlet for this particular, and insistent, aptitude. If you have less of an inclination toward Spatial Visualization, you'll likely gravitate toward activities and careers based on subject matter with less concrete contexts, such as law, counseling, or human resource management. Knowing whether Spatial Visualization is one of your innate abilities will help you to find greater clarity, confidence, and satisfaction throughout your life.

IDEA GENERATION

Do you sometimes find your mind racing? Or interrupt others often? Do you enjoy juggling lots of projects simultaneously? Very likely, your well of ideas never runs dry. Idea Generation is a measure of whether your thoughts go in several directions at once, or are more streamlined. Teachers, journalists, marketers, strategists, salespeople, and many other professionals draw heavily upon this aptitude, which is also known as idea fluency. It is important to remember that Idea Generation indicates the ability to generate a large number of ideas, without any reference to their quality. If this is one of your most prominent aptitudes, you probably love a brainstorming session, public speaking opportunities, or improvisation of any kind. But pay close attention to those who generate ideas more slowly than you; theirs might just be the single best idea. If you are working on a team, make space for their input and be sure to turn to them when it's time to act on a plan, because those for whom this aptitude is less dominant often excel at implementation.

INDUCTIVE REASONING

Have you ever been told you are a good guesser? Do you excel at making decisions under time pressure? Love a good mystery novel or thriller? These are the characteristics of a strong Inductive Reasoner. Inductive Reasoning influences how you approach gathering information and solving problems—that is, how quickly and intentionally you draw conclusions based on the facts available to you. Stock traders, emergency room personnel, private detectives, and game show contestants all enjoy utilizing this natural ability. On the flip side, if you prefer to "sleep on it" or try on a hundred outfits at the mall before you swipe your credit card, you may sit on the other side of this continuum. This reasoning style means you are more comfortable taking your time and working directly with the facts. For example, you might be particularly well suited to work as a hiring manager or a researcher.

Understanding your approach to solving problems, especially novel ones, offers you valuable insight for working on teams, providing leadership, and finding work challenges that you can navigate comfortably.

SEQUENTIAL REASONING

Does your desk sometimes resemble an archaeological excavation site? Do you eschew the value of filing systems, arguing that you can just as easily keep track of things in your head? If you're planning a trip, do you already have it all mapped out, hour by hour, in a logical mental itinerary only you can see? Sequential Reasoning is a problem-solving ability that allows you to mentally arrange information in logical, linear order. As a big-picture logistician, you love to invent systems and sequences. Sequential Reasoners include computer programmers, wedding planners, and logistic professionals, among others. They may view the task of communicating the steps in a process they clearly see in their heads as an unnecessary bother, but the most effective Sequential Reasoners learn to share their systems and plans. After all, being able to communicate a plan is key to gaining followers as well as friends, and even the most brilliant scheme can never materialize if it stays trapped in your brain. Those less inclined to Sequential Reasoning thrive by dedicating themselves to the use of organizational tools such as calendars, schedules, lists, instruction manuals, and filing systems.

In addition to the Core Four, two other aptitudes are critical to recognize and understand. When combined with the core aptitudes, these Amplifiers can have a hefty impact on your overall aptitude profile and the types of work that bring you the greatest fulfillment. The two most important Amplifiers are:

NUMERICAL REASONING

Remember Rebecca, the high school student who declared, before she took her aptitude assessment, that she was not a "math kid"? In traditional school, she struggled in math classes like algebra and geometry. Many people like Rebecca had such a bad experience in school that they spend the rest of their lives avoiding anything with digits, aside from their cell phones. For example, you might have a hidden aptitude for numbers, even though you hated calculus and mathematical theory. Numerical Reasoning simply refers to the ability to logically process complex mathematical problems in daily life. If you have this knack for applying math in order to solve practical problems, you may find, as Rebecca did, that you actually enjoy numerical analysis when it relates directly to some aspect of your life or business. This discovery may, in turn, reveal an untapped potential for working with numbers in applied fields such as data science, engineering, or logistics.

VISUAL COMPARISON SPEED

Are you able to attack a stack of paperwork with ease, efficiency, and accuracy? Do you have a hawklike ability to spot details such as missing commas or misspellings? Visual comparison speed is a measure of visual dexterity that allows you to process written information quickly and with precision. Give a schoolteacher with this aptitude a bright red pen and you get some serious points off if you happen to be a careless student who doesn't double-check your paper for errors. By contrast, if you're a professional who doesn't have a knack for visual comparison speed, you might want to pause before hitting send on an important email. Jobs that rely on this aptitude include lawyers, administrators, editors, auditors, and anything heavily clerical. Understanding where you fall on the continuum of this aptitude can help you efficiently navigate a world full of apartment rental forms, applications, and tax filing documents.

Personality

The study of personality is a fascinating field of psychology with enormous nuance. Over the past century, psychologists have designed a staggering number of instruments to isolate specific personality traits that include a host of subdimensions. Two of these attributes, in particular, are extremely useful in identifying what kinds of roles might best suit you in your chosen career. When combined with knowledge about your aptitudes and interests, your familiarity with these traits and your own personality will allow you to zoom in on the specific careers or projects in which you are likely to excel and avoid those that aren't a good match. The assessment results will reveal key aspects of your personality, including the following:

INTERPERSONAL STYLE

Are you an extrovert, an introvert, or a little of both? Your assessment results will tell you whether you'll thrive working with a team of people or interacting with the public; or whether you'll be happier in a solo endeavor. They can also predict whether remote work will take an emotional toll on you, or do wonders for your mental health.

WORK APPROACH

Are you a "generalist" who looks for opportunities to work with and through others, or a "specialist" who seeks to make contributions that bear the stamp of your individuality? This trait helps determine your work style. Generalists are highly collaborative and happiest when facilitating, managing, or guiding a team toward a shared goal. They tend to be team players with broad skill sets. A specialist derives more satisfaction from being an individual contributor, often playing the role of subject matter expert, and tackling work independently. Of all the cognitive aptitudes and personality traits measured, this one has the least variation: about 75 percent of people are generalists. If you discover in this exercise that you are a specialist, you may understand why at times you have felt like an outlier or at times misunderstood; you probably don't know many people as dedicated as you are to the workings of a Porsche engine or the pros and cons of the Oxford comma.

Interests

The assessment measures your interests based on a brief survey designed to mete out your preferences for a range of activities. Scored on a traditional 1 to 5 scale, it generates a ranking that aligns with clusters of occupations that fall into one of six interest types designated by the acronym RIASEC. These categories are:

REALISTIC

You prefer hands-on work with tangible results. In other words, "doers" are able to point to the results of their labor and say, "See, I built that table!" or "Look at the wonderful improvement in this sick animal I rescued!" Realistic types prefer to use their hands to manipulate aspects of nature, structures, or the physical world.

INVESTIGATIVE

You prefer deep thinking, theoretical contemplation, tough problem-solving, and intellectual inquiry. You love to wrestle with challenges that others haven't yet solved, and you thrive when confronted with tasks such as coming up with a cure to a rare disease, developing a new mathematical formula, or pursuing original insights into a contentious political issue.

ARTISTIC

You enjoy creative pursuits. You may not always feel like creating art, but you have an appreciation for aesthetics and a desire to work in creative environments where your originality is recognized. Not just artists fall into this type; many of the "helping" professions attract artistic personalities because they offer personal inspiration and expression.

SOCIAL

You crave work that will improve the lives of others. You strive to guide, support, help, and advocate on behalf of others, and you gain deep satisfaction from interacting with people. While the social types' aptitudes may, for example, point broadly to the medical field, they will experience greater long-term career satisfaction in areas with high patient interaction and more clinical time, such as psychiatry, natural medicine, or genetic counseling.

ENTERPRISING

You love action, persuasion, and competition. Many competitive athletes rank high in this category and tend to work with particular intensity in all aspects of their lives. Ideal enterprising careers include business, law, and any kind of work that requires meeting deadlines and turning projects around quickly. Enterprising types are also attracted to high-stakes jobs, such as stock broker, news reporter, film director, or fraud examiner.

CONVENTIONAL

You have a preference for activities that are linear, organized, detailed, and orderly. You gravitate toward jobs with clear rules, laws, and structure, particularly situations where there is a concrete right and wrong way to do things. You could feel an immediate pull toward law enforcement or the military, but you may also enjoy less familiar but equally conventional jobs such as paralegal, risk management specialist, auditor, or budget analyst.

What Are My Options for Taking an Aptitude Assessment?

If you bought this book new, you can take the YouScience assessment for free by going to yourhiddengenius.com and entering the unique access code provided with this book. If, on the other hand, you got this book used, you can purchase the test from the YouScience website for $49.

While YouScience is the most comprehensive and affordable assessment of personality, interests, and aptitudes currently available, there are several other options. These include:

- The Johnson O'Connor Research Foundation (https://www.jocrf.org) delivers in-person assessments at eleven different locations throughout the United States. These sessions are administered by a trained coach and some call for the use of paper and pencil. Others may use audio-visual equipment. The final session includes feedback and a summary of your personal assessment delivered by knowledgeable staff. The results generate limited career-matching suggestions and you are provided with general guidance. The cost of this test ranges from $720 to $ 850.
- The Ball Foundation delivers its Career Vision assessment (https://careervision.org/career-vision) on-

line and includes at least one meeting with a career consultant, including follow-up sessions. They offer three assessment packages geared toward career readiness, career launch, early career, and career management and transitions. The costs range from $450 to $1,000.

Braiding It All Together

People who complete the assessment routinely tell us how liberating it is. For the first time in their lives, they can objectively identify where their greatest strengths and challenges lie. This realization not only highlights their untapped potential, it cultivates greater confidence by sharpening their understanding of who they are. At a visceral level, it reveals exactly why you can repeatedly slip into a flow state while participating in certain activities yet can't help getting frustrated or bored with others.

After earning his master's in accountancy, Overton Thompson went to work for one of the world's largest accounting firms. But after just two years, "I was totally burnt out," he recalls. "Calculations that took me hours to figure out seemed to come automatically to many of my colleagues. I always felt like I was playing catch-up. They really got into reviewing the nuances of the tax code." Thompson took his assessment in 2016, and his results pointed to some of the underutilized aptitudes lurking behind his stress. A natural spatial visualizer with a propensity to churn out ideas, he realized the abstract work of accounting would never bring him satisfaction, regardless of his competence. He also saw the incongruence between his extroverted personality and the work he was doing. Days spent in isolation communicating through spreadsheets rather than people were sapping his energy. After some intentional exploration, Thompson joined VaVia, a dumpster rental service, as the director of franchising. Now he is making full use of his natural talents—marketing a physical product, interacting with customers, and writing copy for the website. "And my degree in accounting hasn't gone to waste; it's been a big help to have it as we grow this business," he notes.[4]

When you grasp your full potential, you are free to expand your scope of possibilities and, if you so choose, abandon those frustrating pursuits that have inexplicably refused to bring you any satisfaction, even after years of practice. This knowledge also helps you identify where you are hitting roadblocks in your interpersonal relationships, and how you can become a better team member. At work and at home, you can explore the world around you knowing that your unique assets will lead you to new opportunities and your best, most fulfilled self.

But first, it's helpful to consider how we reached this career-planning juncture in the first place.

From Vocophy to Career Guidance

Centuries will pass 'ere Vocophy is perfected, but time will surely perfect it, for it is a step in the right direction and a long step in the progressive development of our fellow men.

—Lysander Salmon Richards, 1879

The letter from the famous Civil War general William Tecumseh Sherman had just the kind of penmanship Lysander Salmon Richards would expect: tight, flawless, and disciplined.[5] In reply to Richards's request for his opinion on the qualities of a good soldier, Sherman had enclosed a copy of a speech he'd delivered, months earlier, to the 1879 graduating class of the Michigan Military Academy. In the speech, he proclaimed that "war is hell" and emphasized how education and training, alone, cannot compare with what one learns in actual combat.

Later quoting Sherman's letter, Richards added a few other key traits to his vision of the ideal military man. A soldier, he noted, should have "skill with a rifle, habits of abstinence and self-denial, walking long distances, riding on horseback, leaping, running, and all manner of athletic sports," as well as "wisdom and knowledge."[6]

Richards's correspondence with Sherman was one small piece of a broader project to learn about different professions from their most accomplished experts, an apt calling for a man who spent much of his life flitting among diverse vocations. Although he lived well over a century ago, Richards's career path resembled that of many contemporary gig workers. He found employment as a postmaster, justice of the peace, phrenologist (a practitioner who measured skull characteristics to determine a person's health, vocation, and more), businessman, superintendent, politician, and nonprofit manager. A polymath and a visionary, he also wrote books on a constellation of subjects, including *The Beginning and the End of Man*, *The Universe in Brief as I Understand It*, and *Analysis and Cause of the Existence of Memory*.

Drawing upon Sherman's letter, the volume Richards published in 1881 became the first book on the field of career management. Entitled *Vocophy: The New Profession*, it detailed a new and much-needed field whose expert "vocophers" were rigorously trained on the requirements of every known job and used their superior skills in assessing the abilities and interests of individuals to match each person with the most suitable work.

Career Requirements According to a Vocopher

(excerpted from Lysander Richards's 1881 book, *Vocophy: The New Profession*)

Executioner. Should have large destructiveness; must have no fear of death, and be devoid of any sympathy in witnessing suffering in his fellow men. Although it is well to have a small, or perhaps a moderate, amount of brains, yet there is no pursuit that demands an organism more animalistic and so near akin to the brute as that of an executioner.

Hotel Keeper. Must . . . be a good judge of eatables, be neat and know what constitutes a good dinner. Should be very economical but wisely so. If one has inherited a taste for strong drink, it is an obstacle. Must be strong enough to withstand temptations, possessing a great deal of native enterprise and be a good judge of human nature.

Nurse. Should be very quiet and gentle in manner, attentive and interested generally in the comfort and recovery of the sick, the afflicted and maimed. Should be attractive, amiable and kind in attentions, very patient, and not tiresome in conversation. Must be accustomed to confinement, and disturbance during the usual hours of sleep, and withal should be a student of physiology and become familiar with the anatomy and hygiene of the human system to gain success in this worthy and responsible pursuit.

Poet. Prof. Henry Wadsworth Longfellow in a letter to us says: "No one can possibly become a poet without possessing a poetical gift or genius."[7]

In his search for the unique characteristics of each profession, Richards corresponded with hundreds of people and conducted numerous in-person interviews. Using the analog tools at his disposal, he collected as much data as he could and tried to synthesize it, recognizing the potential of such knowledge to change the working world. Though his efforts appear silly and reductive from a modern perspective, the inspiration behind them was revolutionary. Prior to his efforts, most people simply followed in their parents' footsteps or took whatever apprenticeship was available to them. Richards's innovative call to steer people into the most suitable professions broke cleanly from this tradition, yet nearly a century would pass before career guidance began to fulfill its promise.

Soon after publication of his book, actual science began to flourish and a new generation of progressive thinkers began to operationalize a better version of what he had envisioned. In 1907, a new and more promising variation of career guidance emerged spearheaded by Boston social reformer Frank Parsons, who is today widely acknowledged as the "father of career guidance."

In his seminal book, *Choosing a Vocation*, he outlined his approach to vocational consultations, suggesting that the three most important questions a person should ask himself are: "What do I want to do? What am I good at? And if I know what I want to do and what I'm good at, then what are the opportunities for me?"[8] These tenets remain at the heart of career guidance today.

The development of psychometric assessments to objectively measure aptitudes, personality, and interest proliferated between World War I and World War II, funded by both government and industry, which saw the need for matching people with occupations to increase efficiency.

Many psychologists made significant contributions to the field, notably Edward Strong, a young Stanford professor who hypothesized that an inventory of a person's interests would yield a better prediction of his or her future promise in a particular occupation. Outside of the academic arena, Johnson O'Connor, an employee of General Electric, made significant contributions in the study of aptitudes. The suite of tests he developed were initially focused on isolating certain key traits that appeared, over and over, across jobs within the company. By analyzing the natural working aptitudes of the people, instead of the work, he was able to help match individuals to the jobs that best suited them, rather than wedge them into jobs that didn't.

And while IQ and other general intelligence tests grew in popularity, O'Connor continued to emphasize the importance of considering a wide range of abilities. He refused to be limited by the skills others were using to measure "intelligence." Instead, O'Connor argued, we must strive to understand the individual first. "The application of science to the study of man . . . must aim first to prove to each individual that he possesses a unique combination of abilities, one which the world has perhaps never seen before, and one which he can use to new purposes, to create new things, new thoughts," he wrote, "and . . . then show him in what practical, concrete ways he can best use his particular combination of characteristics."[9]

Like Richards and Parsons, O'Connor was a man before his time. His holistic view of individuals foreshadowed late-twentieth-century theories of multiple intelligence types and intellectual competencies. By emphasizing personal strengths and potential over output, he laid the foundation for a whole new understanding of "human resource." One glaring problem remained, however. How could this customized, deeply personal test be scaled up? O'Connor's method for assessing aptitudes was expensive, time-consuming, and required a one-on-one setting that allowed for personalized observation. Given the available technology and the nature of aptitudes, there was no way to deliver these tests on a mass scale or make them accessible to everyone.

Career Guidance in the Digital Age

The notion that we can choose and manage our own careers is relatively new, made possible by the modern market, technology, and increased mobility. While occupations used to last a lifetime and follow predetermined paths based largely on the careers of our parents, the explosion of education and new industries has expanded opportunities, freeing individuals to control their own destinies. With the emergence of the internet and the growing use of personal computers in the 1990s, work began racing to eclipse family, community, and religion as a primary source of meaning and identity in our lives. The boundary between our personal and professional lives began to flicker and fade.[10]

Now, in the twenty-first century, the nature of work is changing so rapidly that we are hard-pressed to keep pace. In the past decade, alone, whole industries have precipitously risen and declined. Technology and automation have swallowed a staggering number of jobs in fields from customer service to manufacturing to medicine; artificial intelligence is set to swallow even more. Real wages have steadily declined, along with union-driven worker protections, and the traditional rewards for job longevity and loyalty have eroded. The days of climbing the corporate ladder and retiring with a gold watch are gone. As secure full-time positions with 401(k)s and medical insurance have mostly disappeared, precarious, no-benefits gig work and perma-lancing have surged, making a comfortable retirement at age sixty or sixty-five increasingly elusive, if not impossible.

Recent studies have revealed a growing demand for social and advanced cognitive skills as well as skill sets well suited to adaptability.[11] Others have identified specific personality traits and interest types that have been shown to thrive in the fast-paced, ever-changing digital workplace.[12] The popular career-based social media site LinkedIn is now using generative artificial intelligence to help both job seekers and recruiters find their best matches. But this new tool is only as good as the data behind it, and for now that includes only the information that can be gleaned from prospective applicants' résumés, social media profiles, and online behavior.[13] Only by mobilizing a person's aptitudes, interests, and personality to identify opportunities and prospective jobs can better, more reliable matches be found. Rooted in our unique and lasting traits, these career picks are also more likely to resist the influence of social biases such as gender stereotypes.[14]

In today's job market, we can't rely on our employers to care for us; we have to care for ourselves. As most of us change jobs, and even industries, multiple times over the course of our careers, we have found it necessary to continually update our skills and reassess our priorities. In order to find satisfaction and success we must constantly evolve with the economy and anticipate jobs that might not yet exist.

At the same time, however, modern innovation has brought new opportunities. As any user of social media knows, predictive algorithms and artificial intelligence have supercharged the ability to sort, sift, and suggest information. With the help of digital technology, we can now aggregate and analyze massive volumes of job and aptitude data. In a matter of years, these developments have brought the century-old vision of viable, accessible, and equitable career guidance closer to realization than ever before. As Dr. Dhanurjay "D.J." Patil, former chief data scientist for the Obama White House, observes: "Data has been a powerful, double-edged sword. On the one hand, it can help match us with a life partner on sites like OkCupid and Bumble; it can aid us in making better healthcare decisions via services like 23andMe and Noom; and it can provide personalized job recommendations via LinkedIn. On the other hand, we need to make sure these services work for everyone and don't cause unintended harm."[15] In our field, the creation of online aptitude assessments has empowered individuals and helped people grasp the full range of their potential futures. But employers should certainly not publicize this information or use it to winnow down pools of job applicants.

In 2012, a company that Betsy cofounded, YouScience, partnered with the Ball Foundation, an aptitude research institution, to launch an online career-matching platform that leverages the internet to expand access to aptitude assessment. YouScience offers a complete suite of tests that measure a person's interests, personality, and, most crucially, aptitudes. It also uses powerful algorithms to generate personalized career matches based on public databases such as the Occupational Information Network (O*NET), a massive storehouse for information on almost every job in America. Unlike its hard copy–only predecessor, the *Dictionary of Occupational Titles*, the O*NET database is an online compilation of in-depth data on current careers throughout the economy.[16] The so-called bible of US occupational data, O*Net serves as a kind of DNA map for employment opportunities. It can be sorted using a search engine and includes a wealth of detailed descriptors for each career. In order to keep this database up to date, psychometricians regularly revise the "occupational fingerprint" of each career based on statistics, technological changes, and ideal aptitude strengths and weaknesses for different activities.

In the third decade of the twenty-first century, Lysander Richards's outlandish predictions about career guidance are beginning to leap, at last, toward reality. Vocophy never caught on, but Richards grasped the future when he imagined a robust system for helping individuals find their most suitable career paths. Unlike our forebears, we now have just the right tools at hand, and with the help of online aptitude assessments, each of us can capture the rich, personalized data we need to better navigate a lifetime of decisions. When we know ourselves we can tackle new work or life transitions with greater assurance, confidence, and direction.

In the next chapter, you'll find the instructions for taking your own assessment, along with a few key tips to guide you through the process. Are you ready to discover your hidden potential?

CHAPTER 2

Ready, Set, Go!

As you become more clear about who you really are, you'll be better able to decide what is best for you, the first time around.
—Oprah Winfrey

Congratulations!

It's time to take your assessment. No preparation or studying is necessary; you only need the time and the willingness to engage in a series of exercises resembling brain games. This "test" will be unlike any you've taken before, and there is no such thing as failure. So, relax, and enjoy.

You will need:

- A desktop or a laptop computer. (The assessment cannot be taken on a mobile or tablet device.)
- One of the following browsers: Safari 7.0 or above, Firefox 38.0 or above, Google Chrome 42.0 or above, or Internet Explorer 10 or above.
- A stable, high-speed, and uninterrupted internet connection. If you are using wireless, please take precautions

because technical difficulties such as an inconsistent internet connection can decrease the accuracy of your results.

- A quiet place, free from distractions, interruptions, alarms, or dings. Before you start, make sure your phone is either off or in silent mode. You're going to need a continuous hour and a half, more or less, of complete peace. We recommend taking a few bathroom or other breaks to let your mind relax between sessions. If you have a busy household, let people know you can't be bothered for ninety minutes. You might even consider putting a Do Not Disturb sign on your door.

- Each exercise takes between five and nine minutes. You are welcome to pause for a break or come back to finish the assessment the next day, but be sure not to click the back button or close your browser during an active exercise.

- When you are ready to take the assessment, go to yourhiddengenius.com and follow the instructions to locate and enter your unique access code. We encourage you to wait until you have your results before you read Chapter 4.

No Judgment!

After taking the assessment, you may feel drained or nervous about your results. Many participants finish with a sour taste in their mouths or the impression that they performed poorly. As one remarked, "I was surprised because after I finished, I thought, *I just completely failed that exercise.* But then I got the results, and discovered that it was one of my strongest aptitudes." Your scores are not "added up"; rather, the goal is to uncover patterns. We are utterly conditioned to equate Low,

Medium, and High with Bad, Better, and Best, but this assessment contains no value judgment and has nothing to do with rankings or accomplishments.

In other words, there is no such thing as acing the assessment. Instead, all of your aptitudes, no matter how strong, point to your range of potential. Think of each aptitude as a continuum. Each position on that continuum has its own unique benefits and challenges, and it's up to you to manage them.

You might experience a rush as you plug away at the brief exercises, especially if you decide not to break them up over time (though you can, and should, take breaks between exercises!). It is also completely normal to feel some frustration or even the sudden impulse to toss your computer out of the window. In fact, you should anticipate some challenges, because the test is designed to push your limits. At times, you may experience a tinge of shame or self-doubt.

It is crucial *not* to view the assessment as a traditional grading system from A+ to F. On the contrary, it resembles an MRI scan that creates a map of your brain, only the assessment generates an image of your innate capabilities. So, if you're haunted by whispers from parents, teachers, or bosses that you're not "good enough, smart enough, or talented enough," remember that this test is a chance to poke holes in that rhetoric and pinpoint all of its flaws.

For some, anxieties can be triggered by any kind of test-like environment. If you do experience this feeling, remember that the assessment is not a tool designed to shut you out; it is meant to welcome you in. Maybe you have taken previous tests that exposed your deficits, but this one will highlight your assets. Thus, "test" is in many ways a misnomer for this assessment, which is instead a kind of looking glass that invites you to grasp your full potential. So, while the process of getting there might be stressful, once you open the envelope to see the gifts within, it will all be worth it.

Exams and assessments had always left McKenna feeling inferior to
her peers. As a result, by age seventeen, she had become apathetic about
school. With bland indifference, she accepted the fact that she would always be the kid needing interventions, support, and accommodations.
When Alex asked her to take a ninety-minute aptitude assessment, you
can imagine McKenna's response. "At first, I thought that it was gonna
be kind of like school, like online school, and I wasn't really going to
have any fun doing it," McKenna told us.[1] At the time, the lingering
effects of the Covid-induced online learning era were uncomfortably
fresh in her mind.

While some of the fourteen sections of the test did cause McKenna
a bit of frustration, she actually enjoyed others. She described having
the unexpected, unfamiliar impression of time flying by during the assessment. That never happened to her while she was doing schoolwork.
She always felt too challenged or too bored, and time seemed to stop.
This was the first time she'd ever flown through a test and felt a spark of
exhilaration when the clock ran out. For McKenna, this was something
entirely new.

We have repeatedly been inspired by observations of young adults
receiving their aptitude results. On one occasion, Betsy remembers the
students sitting in their chairs expectantly. Some fidgeted while others
glanced nervously at their neighbors. But as their assessment reports
popped up on their computer screens, a transformation took place.
Each student became extremely focused on their online report and, as
they read, their backs collectively straightened, as if their lungs were expanding with possibility. They looked like flowers in a time-lapse video,
extending each petal to greet the sun. It was so moving to see them open
their eyes and start viewing themselves differently. At that moment,
each one caught sight of the potential that other people had already
seen in them, but until now, they themselves had been unable to recognize it. It was life-changing. We want you to have the same experience.

Your Results Dashboard

After completing your assessment, give yourself time to process the experience, decompress, and absorb your results with a fresh and open mind.

You'll be able to view your results in two formats: (1) on your personal YouScience dashboard, and (2) in a printable report (look for the green button). You'll also have access to a valuable discussion guide containing key words and phrases that describe you. This will help you craft a résumé, an online profile, a personal statement, and interview points.

Your online dashboard is rich with occupational information. Be sure to use the sorting buttons on the dashboard to view your personalized career suggestions based on your "aptitude only" fits versus your "interest only" fits. These are often quite different. The algorithms that generate these matches are developed by leading industrial and organizational psychologists who use the most comprehensive career data sourced from O*NET, the Bureau of Labor Statistics, and the US Department of Education's National Center for Education Statistics.

Your "Aha" Moment

Your assessment results will offer insight into not just your ideal career options, but how you are prone to approach everyday tasks at home and in interactions with others. Some test takers find their own intuitions confirmed while others are surprised, but all find themselves newly equipped with the language and confidence to reevaluate and pursue greater fulfillment. Our hope is that your results will open up new pathways and initiate a journey of exploration and discovery.

While the density and complexity of your results may feel overwhelming at first, we encourage you to take your time. It's a lot of information to process, including the subtle synergies between the Core Four and the Amplifiers. We recommend you download your profile and put it somewhere accessible so you can refer back to it easily, as you gradually process its contents. In these weeks after receiving your results, you'll become more attuned to your untapped potential and will begin to internalize your personal profile of aptitudes, personality traits, and interests, and what they mean for your life's work.

The YouScience algorithm also matches your aptitude profile, certain personality traits, and your personal interests to specific careers, inviting you to explore how your newfound knowledge can guide your choice of work.[2] Ideally, when it comes to paid work, you want to find the sweet spot at the intersection of your natural talents and the array of occupations most closely aligned with them. Later on in this book, after you've reviewed your unique profile, we will walk you through how to best interpret your career recommendations based on your core driving aptitudes. Each chapter dedicated to one of these aptitudes contains historical context, case studies, research, and opportunities for use that will help you evaluate their role in your own life.

In the following pages, you will meet amazing people who have discovered their hidden genius. Their unique personality characteristics and core aptitudes are clearly evident in their work and skills, anchoring the satisfaction they find in their daily lives. Through these stories and your own experience, you will witness how this awareness brings with it the confidence to cast off any doubts that may be preventing you from living your most fulfilling life. Have fun with the assessment exercises, and we'll see you on the other side!

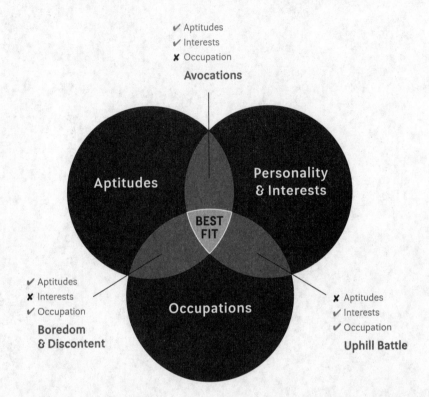

Best-fit occupations lie at the intersection of what we are both good at and enjoy doing. Careers that fit only our aptitudes may leave us feeling uninspired or working in the wrong context. Careers that only fit our interests and personality traits will, over time, leave us feeling either bored if our aptitudes are not engaged, or overwhelmed if our aptitudes are not a match for the work. Careers that are a good fit for our aptitudes but may be unavailable to us due to external factors are avocations, rather than revenue-generating vocations.

Part II

Your Core Four

Try this. Grab a pen and a piece of paper, and hold the pen in your nondominant hand. Already, that might feel a bit awkward. Now write your full name. How does it look? More important, how did it feel?

Switch hands and write your name again with your dominant hand. Unless you are ambidextrous, this will be a lot easier. Even though writing feels totally natural for our dominant hands, something as simple and routine as writing our names can be a challenge for the other hand. Much like your dominant hand, your aptitudes reflect your natural potential for certain types of activities.

In 1902, a naturally left-handed seven-year-old boy who was forced to write with his right hand started to develop a severe stutter. That boy was England's Duke of York, the future King George VI, and the father of Queen Elizabeth II. Prince George's left-hand preference was seen, in the early twentieth century, as a biological anomaly associated with deviancy—a tendency absolutely unthinkable in a prince. But even as George stumbled through forced right-handedness, a few psychologists began to notice a pattern among retrained left-handers. The left-handers demonstrated a condition known as "misplaced sinister," evidenced by stammering.[1] Experimentation, observation, and more reliable information showed that speech impediments, along with a slew of other learning challenges, sprang up among children forced to use their nondominant hand.

Why would left-handedness require such unnecessary and torturous discipline? The reason lies in ancient social norms. For centuries, left-handers were stigmatized—branded as incipiently insane at best, or, at worst, associated with the devil.[2] (The word *sinister* comes from the Latin for "on the left side.") Comprising only about 10 percent of the population, left-handers were ostracized and accused of witchcraft.[3]

Imagine the slow, awkward, and often frustrating reality of having to constantly learn new things with your nondominant hand. Eventually, through grueling practice, that hand might become conventionally useful. But forcefully neglecting your natural preference would mean you may not be realizing your full potential. Your nondominant hand will never become dominant. And why would you want it to? Forcing yourself to use it at school, work, and play would eventually fatigue you and hold you back; you'd work harder for no reason other than to say you did it. What's the point of that?

The most promising activities are the "dominant hand" ones for which you have some natural inclination. Frequently engaging in these activities allows you to find the satisfaction and happiness that comes from feeling "in the zone," and finding a career that uses them will help you find fulfillment. By contrast, if most of your activities do not engage your aptitudes, or if you are constantly working to develop skills not aligned with them, you are essentially holding your pen in the wrong hand. Get ready to deepen your understanding of your inherent qualities, celebrate them, and put them to work.

CHAPTER 3

Spatial Visualization

Everyone has two eyes, but no two people have the same view.
—Anonymous

SPATIAL VISUALIZATION

Abstract Thinker	⟨ ⟨ ⟨ ⟨ ⟨	Space Planner	⟩ ⟩ ⟩ ⟩ ⟩	3D Visualizer

On November 26, 2020, in the middle of the Covid-19 pandemic, more than a few cooped-up New Yorkers left their apartments and hurried down Thirty-Fourth Street toward Macy's department store in Herald Square. They'd gotten a glimpse on their TVs of the marching bands, acrobats, Broadway performers, celebrities, and enormous balloons that make up the iconic Macy's Thanksgiving Day Parade and were rushing, as New Yorkers are wont to do, to catch the real thing as it happened. For nearly a century, the parade has served as the unofficial kickoff to the holiday season, drawing millions of TV viewers and as many as 3.5 million in-person onlookers, who line the wide avenues of Manhattan to watch the spectacle unfold.

In 2020, no doubt to their great disappointment, the locals who rushed out into the unusually quiet streets saw . . . not much. In September, fearing the pandemic disaster that could ensue if masses of people were to crowd together, city officials had canceled the parade. There were no roaring crowds, no marching bands, and only a handful of balloons. Police barricades kept the streets surrounding Macy's virtually empty. "I saw half a balloon," one bystander told the *New York Times*. "If I stayed home, I would have seen more of the parade."[1]

It's true. If you were among the 22 million people watching that day on television, you likely wouldn't have known anything was amiss. On-screen, the parade appeared to be going on in full force, just like every other year.

It was a spectacular optical illusion.

One by one, during the three days leading up to Thanksgiving, costumed parade acts had come to a cordoned-off section in front of Macy's to be videotaped marching down that single block. On Thanksgiving morning, the production team were holed up in a trailer, linking together these prerecorded segments with footage of the smattering of balloons and floats going down the block in real time to create the seamless spectacle viewers saw on their screens.

This digital miracle on Thirty-Fourth Street proves that the team was well stocked with 3D Visualizers—folks who find it exceptionally easy to imagine objects in three-dimensional space, like rotating a Rubik's Cube in their heads. The producers could take the micro-snippets of this massive performance and quickly see how they best fit together, break it all down into its tiniest parts and mentally reassemble them into one coherent experience. They could envision the parade from every angle: through the eyes of the performers, through the television camera technicians' lenses, from the overhead perspective of camera drones that show no mercy to an out-of-place marching band member, and from the points of view of the New Yorkers who watch the parade at every level, starting down on the sidewalk and soaring all the way up to the private terraces of penthouse apartments. They could picture the last second of the previous act and the first second of the next act, and then fast-forward and rewind the Rockettes' routine. And this time, like they must every year, they did it all without a dress rehearsal, because there's no shutting down a Manhattan street just for practice.

Spatial Visualization describes the ease or difficulty with which you can imagine objects in three dimensions. If, like a parade producer, you can mentally rotate objects and picture them from multiple angles and perspectives, you're probably drawn to physical, concrete work. The options for your career are broad including building, design, choreography, and manufacturing to name a few. Hands-on hobbies as varied as golf or LEGO competitions may satisfy you if your profession offers too few opportunities to exercise this aptitude. In one inspiring instance, a renowned investment adviser surprised us by winning a national ballroom dance competition, demonstrating how to balance office work with nimble footwork. The fact is, Spatial Visualization is an aptitude that demands attention and use. Leave it unattended and you're almost certain to feel a little frustrated, like a racehorse that isn't allowed to run.

That's why it's important to know whether you are a 3D Visualizer. If you are, you have a number of career options you may never have considered. And if you aren't? That's fine, too.

Picture Your Breakfast

The study of what psychometricians call spatial ability began in Victorian England with the work of Francis Galton, an intellectual and inventor.[2] Galton's research and contributions to a number of scientific fields are vast and disparate; he invented the pressure-system weather map and introduced the statistical concepts of correlation and regression.

Inspired by the work of his half cousin Charles Darwin, Galton spent years studying various human abilities and devising tests to measure them. His methods were hardly scientifically rigorous; in fact, they seemed intentionally designed to prove his hypothesis that traits such as intelligence were purely hereditary. He concluded that people from his own privileged class of white males belonged to a more "able race" born with a natural "masculine intellectual superiority."[3]

Notwithstanding these obvious offenses, Galton also devised a test to assess the human capacity for what he called "Mental Imagery": he asked subjects to close their eyes and imagine their breakfast table. What objects could they recall? Was the image in their memory vivid and clear or vague and murky? Could they clearly distinguish "the colours of the china, of the toast, bread-crust, mustard, meat, parsley" or other items on the table?[4] Because his experiment relied on study subjects to self-report, it would not pass muster today. Still, Galton's inquiries mark the earliest effort to study Spatial Visualization.

Beginning in 1940, American men between the ages of twenty and forty-five were required to register for the draft. Those selected by lottery were sent to serve in the US armed forces. Seeking an efficient way to match these untrained recruits from diverse backgrounds into the jobs most suitable for them, the military launched a new program of widespread aptitude assessment. For example, the United States Army Air Forces administered its Aviation Cadet Qualifying Exam to assess recruits for the "physical fitness, the mental alertness, the personal daring to meet the acid test of air crews for high-powered military aircraft."[5]

In 1943, a brochure for the exam breathlessly explained how each candidate's mathematical ability, vocabulary, reading and mechanical comprehension, "alertness to recent happenings," and practical judgment were measured.[6] As noted in a 1942 Army Air Forces report on the exam's purpose, development, and validation:

This section contains a number of diagrams, pictures, or perspective drawings. . . . The diagrams are largely self-explanatory so that individuals with good aptitude but with no training in mechanics or mechanical drawing and no previous experience with the devices portrayed can select the correct answers to the questions. All essential parts are labeled, so that a man unfamiliar with conventional drawing symbols can identify fixed and movable parts, bearings, openings, etc. Machines or devices with which some individuals could be expected to be very familiar are not used.

This section measures the ability to comprehend spatial relations, the ability to understand mechanical movements, pressure relations, and the principles of operations of simple mechanical devices. It measures chiefly non-verbal ability and favors men with natural mechanical aptitude.[7]

A man's performance on this assessment proved to be the second-best indicator—coming in just behind sound judgment—of his potential success in the most prestigious spot on an aircrew: the pilot. Strong mechanical comprehension scores also correlated with success as a bombardier (the crew member responsible for targeting and destroying enemy missiles barreling through the sky toward the aircraft) or a navigator.

During this period, researchers also identified several sub-facets of spatial ability, as well. These include mental rotation (think jigsaw puzzles, Tetris, and, of course, the Rubik's Cube); spatial perception, or the ability to determine the relationship of your body position to the position of other objects; and spatial working memory, or the ability to recall landmarks along a route you're about to drive (as well as where in the world you last set down your car keys).

The Exercise

The assessment we use deploys the most common and accepted measurement of Spatial Visualization, developed and published by the Educational Testing Service in the 1970s. It is called the "paper-folding exercise," but the only folding that's happening is in your imagination. You'll see a series of diagrams. Each one represents a rectangular piece of paper that has been folded in a different way and punched with an imaginary hole-puncher. You'll be asked to picture where the punched holes would appear if the paper were to be unfolded and laid flat. As the assessment continues, the examples become increasingly complex.

Try it yourself with this example:

MENTAL PAPER FOLDING
A piece of paper has been folded and hole punched.
Which numbered image corresponds to the folded paper?

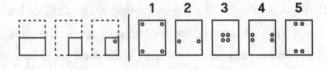

The amount of effort it took you to determine the answer (number 4) holds a clue to your visualization style.

Of the test takers YouScience has assessed since 2010, the largest number, about 45 percent, find the paper-folding exercise challenging, but not impossible. They don't immediately see the answer but can work out the solution given enough time; they're the people in the middle of the Spatial Visualization continuum, whom we call Space Planners. About 25 percent of takers become exceedingly frustrated, often to the point of giving up; these are the Abstract Thinkers. Then there are the

30 percent who are able to spot the answers almost effortlessly and even find the paper-folding exercise fun. They're the 3D Visualizers.

The 3D Visualizer

Although it is a core aptitude, Spatial Visualization often goes unrecognized in traditional school settings. According to Vanderbilt University psychologists Gregory Park, David Lubinski, and Camilla P. Benbow, identifying and acknowledging young people with this aptitude could help steer more people into in-demand STEM careers.[8] If you're assessed as a 3D Visualizer, you could also have strong math skills: research indicates that there's some overlap in the parts of the brain associated with math and mental rotation.[9]

If you're a 3D Visualizer, you're generally able to interpret diagrams and blueprints easily. When you're lost and consulting a map, trying to figure out how to get back to the freeway, you don't have to physically rotate the map so it faces the same direction you're facing. You're at a distinct advantage on projects that involve placing or reorganizing objects, such as designing a garden makeover or arranging your living room furniture in a new home. When trying to process a new concept, you may sketch it out. In fact, you prefer pictures, tables, and figures to written text. You also prefer to work with and think about real things, such as tools, products, and buildings. But it isn't just inanimate objects: for the producers of the Macy's Thanksgiving Day Parade, the three-dimensional "things" they work with are human beings on a collection of city blocks.

Bolingbrook, Illinois, firefighter Nicole McGowan uses her aptitude for Spatial Visualization in a number of ways, depending on the work she is doing. McGowan had always wanted to be in what she calls "a helping people career" and considered physical therapy, nursing, and athletic training before deciding to join the fire service.[10] Even before her assessment results identified her as a 3D Visualizer, she instinctively chose a career that's an excellent fit. Called to a burning building, McGowan can picture the way smoke will travel through open or closed doors and windows as she considers how to safely enter and exit. When she conducts an inspection to help a contractor make a building as fireproof as possible, McGowan can envision the hidden sprinkler and ventilation systems and understand whether the necessary fire alarms are located in the proper spots.

3D Visualizer Challenges

Challenges with abstract thinking are common among 3D Visualizers. If, as a student, you felt drained when listening to lectures and reading textbooks, but energized when your homework involved creating a diorama, your aptitude for Spatial Visualization was making itself known. If these kinds of assignments were few and far between, that's because, by and large, conventional teaching methods favor abstract learners. As a result, 3D Visualizers may struggle in school.

America's educational system relies on verbal and quantitative tests that don't paint a sufficient picture of students' cognitive diversity. This can leave talented 3D Visualizers feeling like failures and cause their grades to suffer. While, for example, they can call upon their ability to visualize a cell and its structures during a biology test, they may have trouble completing the homework assignments that require them to learn the names of all of the cell's components.

As a result, many 3D Visualizers fall through the cracks. In fact, in the early twentieth century, when Stanford's Lewis Terman set out to identify and study the smartest children in California—those whose Stanford-

Binet IQ test scores put them in the top 1 percent of intelligence—among the children who took the test but didn't make the "genius" cutoff was Luis Walter Alvarez.

Alvarez grew up to win the Nobel Prize in physics for developing methods to record and analyze particle interactions. Separately, with his son Walter Alvarez, an earth and planetary science professor at the University of California, Berkeley, he came up with the now widely accepted theory that an asteroid collision was the cause of the mass extinction of the dinosaurs. Recent research suggests that the secret sauce behind his genius was his ability to think in 3D; a talent that Terman's IQ test didn't measure.

Of course, we believe that widespread aptitude testing among students would identify 3D Visualizers early and help them get the attention they deserve and the learning techniques that would set them up for success. For McKenna (whom you met in Chapter 2), an essay writing technique developed to help students with dyslexia worked like a charm given her score as a 3D Visualizer. The technique involves organizing information into a visual chart. "I just fill it out," she says, "and within five minutes, all of a sudden, my whole essay is done." Like a map, recipe, or diagram, the visual guide makes an abstract activity more concrete.

In the summer of 2020, as the Covid-19 pandemic marooned millions of teenagers at home with few outlets for entertainment, McKenna discovered a new passion: real estate. "One of the first things to open up were model homes," she says. "Each morning, I would sit down and look up available listings. Then my friend and I would just literally go and look at all the open houses we could." McKenna's friend eventually got tired of the activity, but McKenna was hooked. After touring every available home in her area, she began driving out of town to look at residential listings beyond the city limits. McKenna's obsession with real estate isn't coincidental: it lines up perfectly with her aptitude for Spatial Visualization.[11]

If you're a 3D Visualizer employed in an abstract field, you don't necessarily need to toss out your career and start over. Perhaps there are features of your current role, including certain daily tasks and aspects of your work environment, that satisfy your three-dimensional mind.

Jonas Sorensen,[12] who is studying to become a Lutheran minister, couldn't have chosen a more abstract career despite his aptitude for Spatial Visualization; clergy members and theologians devote their lives to the otherworldly, the intangible, and the spiritual. But Sorensen is also drawn to the physicality of religious worship.

"In the Lutheran service there is choreography," he says. "It involves incense, robes, bells, candles, sanctuaries, musical cues, amens, hallelujahs, and a whole lot of kneeling, standing and genuflecting." The architecture of the church—those high-vaulted ceilings, representing the divine, that draw the eye upward from the human, earthly plane—also appeals to Sorensen. Churches, he says, are "spatially delicious."[13]

It goes to show that if you're drawn to a field that seems counter to your visualization style—or any other of the Core Four aptitudes—you may be able to find approaches to your work that satisfy your innate abilities.

3D Visualizers at Work

Park, Lubinski, and Benbow point to studies that show people with a strong 3D Visualization style tend to do well in the physical sciences, computer science, engineering, and math. For 3D Visualizers who prefer face-to-face interaction over solo time in a science lab, fields including urban planning, international development, and economics can be a good fit. On average, this aptitude is highest in architects, mechanical and electrical engineers, computer programmers, carpenters, and machinists, but there are numerous, sometimes surprising ways to use your three-dimensional gift.

3D Visualizers who are college students and aren't particularly interested in the fields well suited to this aptitude might consider an interdisciplinary major such as physics and philosophy; or science, technology, and society. Some students excel in science but don't love the idea of exclusively studying it, or they're interested in medicine but don't really want to be doctors. Instead, they may light up when they learn about fields like public health, genetic counseling, and healthcare administration—all of which have a concrete, real-world component.

Whatever your aptitude profile, no job can make use of every aptitude, all of the time. That's where leisure activities come in. For example, certain physical, intellectual, and creative pastimes that include a heavy three-dimensional component can help satisfy your need to work with concrete objects. (See the Appendix for more examples of job types and other activities that align with 3D Visualization.)

The Abstract Thinker

On the opposite side of the Spatial Visualization continuum are Abstract Thinkers who relate more readily to work involving concepts, ideas, feelings, or stories than to work involving physical spaces or material objects.

If Nicole McGowan is a classic 3D Visualizer, Nadine Cipriani is her visualization-style opposite. A business development executive at the global consulting firm Ernst & Young (EY), Cipriani supports federal clients with modernization and transformation efforts. Cipriani began her twenty-year career in the accounting department at a corporation that provided information technology services to commercial and federal clients.

"After a few weeks performing dry and uninspiring calculations, I wondered why I was only being asked to calculate overhead rates"—

the cost of running a business that doesn't lead to profits, such as insurance, licenses, and rent. Cipriani couldn't understand, she says, why "no one seemed to care about the underlying reasons for their wide swings." She began calling the company's branch offices and departments to figure out the "why" behind the numbers. Ultimately, she created an analysis to present to the controller that explained, "'Hey, by the way, your overhead rates are going up and down because of these variables,'" she says.[14] Her ability to imagine intangibles is a key contributor to her success.

Roughly a quarter of the population processes information by hearing it, reading it, and talking it through, without diagrams or other visual aids. Abstract Thinkers have little trouble wrapping their minds around the emotions, feelings, and memories that a 3D Visualizer can find hard to grasp. Abstract Thinkers philosophize and daydream. They are adept at listening, reflecting, synthesizing, and communicating their thoughts. They gravitate toward the humanities and liberal arts, undeterred by the subjectivity and gray areas in those disciplines.

Sue Joyce has harnessed her Abstract Thinking ability as the founder of a business that at first glance would seem a better fit for a 3D Visualizer, her aptitude opposite. Joyce's company, Turkish-T, sells a luxury brand of handcrafted textiles. Popular among millennials and baby boomers alike, the brand appeals to cotton purists who value quality as well as style. A 3D Visualizer might have begun as a textile artist and built a company from there. But Joyce, a former buyer for a gift shop, shaped the business from an entirely different direction. Driven by a desire to create a marketplace for women-made artisanal goods, she landed upon a sustainable product—cotton towels—and then carefully researched how to bring it to life. Drawn into the history of the peshtemal, the traditional textile used in the Turkish hammam (bathhouses), she wanted to reintroduce it into modern homes. Her ability to tell the story transformed a simple towel into an object of desire. She draws satisfaction knowing hundreds of female artisans are making a living using their skill in ancient looming techniques. "I had a sense of what people wanted and I saw there was a gap in the market," Joyce says, "and it took me about three years to pull everything together."

This is what Abstract Thinkers can do so well: use story to elevate the physical to the ephemeral. They easily grasp concepts involving ideas and feelings. They're adept at navigating relationships, observing body language, and understanding people's emotional motivations.

Abstract Thinker Challenges

Even if you didn't know until now that 3D Visualizers existed, if you're an Abstract Thinker, you likely weren't surprised that the paper-folding exercise drove you mad.

A person who primarily learns and expresses themselves verbally generally doesn't mind not being much of a 3D Visualizer and has figured out workarounds when tackling problems in the physical world. You might pay to have your IKEA furniture preassembled. Rather than trying to make perfect roses from icing, you order a birthday cake from the bakery.

"I'm terrible when it comes to directions," Cipriani admits with a laugh, remembering a regular walk she used to take with a friend when she was in her twenties. "We would meet up each week, but whenever the seasons changed, I would be late or get lost—even though the route stayed the same." Cipriani doesn't hold a mental map in her head the way a 3D Visualizer might, so she compensated by relying on a visual landmark: she knew, when she saw a particular tree, to make a right turn to meet her walking buddy. "When the tree changed colors in the fall, I'd get confused and miss the turn. And then once I finally got it, and winter came, I'd get lost again. Then when the leaves came back in the spring, I was lost all over again." Today Cipriani relies on Waze and Google Maps, so she can focus her attention on the skills at which she naturally shines.

At the same time, Abstract Thinkers would do well to remember that some co-workers, friends, or family members may not be as comfortable learning or communicating at their level of verbal prowess. Be aware that some of the people around you have an entirely opposite way of approaching the world—and that's a good thing, because their strengths can complement yours. These are the people, after all, who can read the map.

Abstract Thinkers at Work

Research shows that educators, counselors, lawyers, and many people in business tend to score further toward the abstract side of the Spatial Visualization continuum. In their leisure time, Abstract Thinkers may find themselves drawn to activities as varied as meditation, travel to historic sites, individual sports, political activism, and game theory. (See the Appendix for more examples of job types and other activities that align with Abstract Thinking.)

The Space Planner

If your profile lands you in the middle of the Spatial Visualization continuum, you might be able to study an object and then, with concentration or practice, envision it in space. You can take or leave hands-on endeavors, and you can work comfortably with both theories and their applications.

Olivia Mason, a certified sommelier (a trained wine steward) in London, has a role that perfectly straddles the abstract and concrete worlds. For several years, she worked in vineyards in California, New Zealand, and Oregon, learning every aspect of wine production: from sorting grapes in the vineyard to maintaining a stable environment for fermentation to managing the tasting room. "Everything except picking the grapes," she says. From these experiences, she realized that she much preferred explaining the hands-on process of winemaking to doing it herself. "I loved describing the many inputs that go into a great bottle of wine," she says.[15]

Today, Mason works for a wine and wine-lifestyle media brand that hosts a renowned annual winemaking competition. She writes about the award winners for a global audience of oenophiles. Keenly aware of the tangible process and products that make up the world of wine, Mason has found her niche in sharing the experience through words.

The 45 percent of people who, like Mason, score toward the middle of the Spatial Visualization continuum can enjoy working with objects and on projects with tangible outcomes, but their work doesn't need a three-dimensional component to be fulfilling. A Space Planner may be in their element in an administrative role that also includes a little hands-on creativity, such as event planning; or in a communications role, such as technical writing that requires knowing about objects or processes and also explaining them to others.

Space Planners can visualize in three dimensions, but not automatically or effortlessly. Instead, they employ a more deliberate step-by-step mental process. Because they live between both worlds, it's not uncommon for them to stumble a bit before discovering a role that taps their gifts without being overly concrete or abstract.

It took Brianna Bullentini a few tries. Bullentini grew up in Reno and is the daughter and granddaughter of construction workers. When she was young, her dad would regularly bring her along to his jobs, and to this day, the smell of a construction site—the paint, concrete, and wood—makes her nostalgic; she still gets excited about it.

She didn't love school, but she did love playing high school football; she was, and remains, the only female all-regional wide receiver in the state of Nevada. Initially resistant to the idea of college, she agreed to apply to architecture school when her parents insisted, but with a caveat. She'd only apply to a "reach" school, Parsons School of Design, and if she got in, she'd go. To her surprise, she was accepted. It turns out her football career made her a standout.

Bullentini earned her degree, but it wasn't easy. "I didn't belong there," she says. She didn't enjoy studying the essential aspects of building construction: elevation, grade and altitude, and other topics. What fascinates her is the way humans interact with their environment. "I'm interested in the anthropology of it all. Yes, you're building buildings, but you're building for people—you're putting walls around the psychology of people."

Now a strategy consultant for a real estate developer, Bullentini helps designers and architects with the practical, human parts of large projects—details such as where the parking should be. Her role exercises both sides of the Spatial Visualization continuum: she understands blueprints and building plans but can also step back and ask, "How will neighbors interact in this space?" and "Will people be happy here?"[16]

Space Planner Challenges

When Bullentini received her aptitude profile, she was finally able to verbalize what she'd been feeling for years. She has three-dimensional awareness—giving her a designer's eye, a football player's edge, and an architect's interest in tangible work—but she doesn't reside on that end of the continuum. She remembers the paper-folding exercise being harder than she'd thought it would be. "I wanted to literally fold a piece of paper I had next to me because I would have felt more comfortable doing it in physical form," she says. Instead, "I walked through the folding cadence in my head, step by step."[17]

Space Planners at Work

If you fall in the middle of the Spatial Visualization continuum, you'll be comfortable with work that includes production or has other concrete aspects, but you'll probably gravitate toward a supporting role in the products' design or execution. Your intermediate ability is expressed in professions including sales, real estate, manufacturing, construction, and social media marketing. Space Planners also enjoy a range of pastimes, from the highly physical, such as sporting events, to the theoretical, such as political debates. (See the Appendix for more examples of job types and other activities that align with those who score as Space Planners.)

Crafting the Strongest Hand

In his book *The Pathfinder*, Nicholas Lore writes: "Mother Nature dealt each of us a very specific hand of natural talent and personality cards. Throughout our lives, we play various combinations of these cards in our work and elsewhere."[18] Only by recognizing and consulting these cards can we play them dynamically, adapting ourselves to different tasks and opportunities. Like the other core drivers, visualization style has the exceptional power of an ace or a face card in your own personal deck of cards. But in cards as in the game of life, the combinations you choose to create with your hand make all the difference. For example, you might have a ten, a jack, a king, and an ace of diamonds, which might be useful. But it depends on your other cards. If you also have the queen of diamonds, you'll have something truly impressive: a straight flush. Knowing your other core aptitudes allows you to craft your strongest hand.

CHAPTER 4

Idea Generation

Ideas are like rabbits. You get a couple and learn how to handle them, and pretty soon you have a dozen.

—John Steinbeck

IDEA GENERATION

Concentrated
Focuser ⟨ ⟨ ⟨ ⟨ ⟨ Idea
Contributor ⟩ ⟩ ⟩ ⟩ ⟩ Brainstormer

"Don't worry, your things will be safe." The guard at the Debra K. Johnson Rehabilitation Center, a women's prison in Tennessee, nodded cheerfully as she took Pat Shea's handbag and wrote down the contents—wallet, cell phone, and keys—on a bright yellow form. Then she scanned Shea with a wand from head to toe.

With a twinge of apprehension, Shea walked through the prison entrance. As she heard the door lock behind her, she reminded herself how happy she was to be there. What better way to recognize the special gift these women had given her nonprofit?

As the CEO of the Nashville YWCA, Shea was visiting the prison for a photo op. The inmates had recently donated ninety-three dollars to her organization's domestic violence shelter, a significant amount from the prisoners' perspectives. With prison jobs that pay less than a dollar, on average, for a full day's work, the effort had required serious coordination and commitment. It was spearheaded by Gaile Owens, a victim of prolonged domestic violence who had hired a stranger to kill her abusive husband (the governor later commuted her sentence and she was granted parole). Shea was deeply moved by the women's collective sacrifice, as well as their shared trauma.

A uniformed guard escorted Shea to an auditorium with hundreds of chairs in tight rows. Yolanda Walker, the prison chaplain greeted her with a warm smile.

"Mrs. Shea? We are so happy to have you with us today," said Walker. "We've given you an hour to speak. Is that enough time?"

Shea's eyes widened. "What?"

"You're today's guest speaker. Didn't the warden tell you? The women are so excited to hear what you have to say!"

Shea hadn't prepared to say anything at all, but she quickly composed herself. A few minutes later, she walked to the podium and tested the microphone as three hundred convicted felons filed into the auditorium. "The next ninety minutes," Shea told us, "were among the most exhilarating of my life."

Looking out over the assembly of women clad in pale blue Tennessee Department of Correction uniforms, Shea asked for a show of hands. "Who here has been the victim of domestic violence?" Nearly everyone raised their hands. Shea could feel the connection among the women surge like an electric current. From the front of the room, she began talking about womanhood, pain, and resilience, drawing upon her years of experience serving the victims of domestic violence at the YWCA. Then she invited the prisoners to share their stories, and her talk turned into a more free-flowing conversation. "The best part was improvising and engaging with the audience," she remembered. In fact, Shea believes that her lack of preparation actually made her talk *better*. "I really felt in the zone," she said. "There was so much participation, and the women asked so many important questions."

To some, the situation Shea faced would feel paralyzing. But for her, it sparked enthusiasm, spurring ideas and helping her improvise. Although she began with the kind of talk she'd given many times before, she quickly adapted to the audience, pulling off her impromptu speech with courage, compassion, and aplomb.

Years later, when Shea received her aptitude assessment results, she immediately identified with the description of her own Idea Generation score as a Brainstormer. "Whether it was in my first job, getting to know the families on my 'paperboy' route or waiting tables in high school and college, I was able to talk to just about anyone about anything. I grew up in a large family, one of eight children, in Wheeling, West Virginia," she went on to explain, "I had to wait my turn in order to get a word in at dinner. In our home, conversation was the entertainment so it helped if you were able to think on your feet."[1]

Brainstormers like Shea excel at generating ideas in rapid succession, on command, regardless of time, place, or topic. In unexpected situations, their brains behave like improvisational dancers, moving effortlessly without rehearsal or practice. By contrast, filtering ideas or taking time to test their merits is secondary for them. Falling on the right-hand side of the Idea Generation continuum means that you are able to produce a massive quantity, though not necessarily the greatest quality, of brainchildren.

At the other extreme, Concentrated Focusers are more inclined to produce one idea at a time and only share their thoughts after careful evaluation. Before speaking up, they always ask themselves, "Is my opinion viable?" Spared from the potential distraction of too many ideas, they excel at implementing and following through. They draw great satisfaction from executing a winning concept, regardless of who thought of it.

Idea Contributors sit in the middle of the Idea Generation continuum. When something sparks their interest or engages one of their passions, their inspiration flows quickly and easily. They prefer to keep the end goal in view, and they may jump in as referees when a roomful of Brainstormers wanders off on too many tangents. They're also good at recognizing when it's time to stem the flow of ideas, take stock, and move the group toward a promising game plan.

The concepts of brainstorming and idea rate are both relatively new, with roots buried deep in psychology and early understandings of creativity. The story of how they emerged, and how they came to be measured, offers insight into why the Idea Generation aptitude is so important to your self-discovery.

From Gobolinks to Rap Battling

The first seed for the testing of Idea Generation was planted in the late nineteenth century when science and creativity collided in an obscure art form known as "klecksography." The original klecksographs, or symmetrical inkblot images, were printed in a book of poetry by German physician Justinus Kerner. In America, they were popularized as "gobolinks" or inkblot "shadow pictures" that inspired whimsical, often nonsensical verse. The authors of the first printed gobolink collection invited their readers to "drift for a while among goblins and elves" and rediscover the creative imagination of childhood.[2]

In Europe, these images gave rise to a game known as "Klecksographie," in which children collected inkblot cards to use in telling stories and making imaginative connections. One Swiss boy named Hermann Rorschach became so enamored of klecksographs that his friends called him "Kleck." As a young psychologist in the 1920s, Rorschach created a new test and claimed he could diagnose schizophrenia based on a person's response to ten different, standardized inkblot images.[3]

Around the same time, British psychologist Graham Wallas began exploring "idea fluency," or the number of ideas a person can generate, as part of the developmental process that leads to creativity. Other psychologists emphasized the need to more clearly distinguish these elements, because creativity depends on sustained spontaneity and deviation, rather than idea volume. Here, too, images and drawings were popular tools for gauging different types of inspiration. As American psychologist Ray Simpson wrote: "A person might be pregnant with new combinations of ideas, and yet they would not have any special significance as being useful, artistic or unique."[4] Thirty years later, psychologist J. P. Guilford defined divergent thinking as the ability to produce a variety of ideas or alternatives when presented with a challenge. Subsequent tests of divergent thinking examined different characteristics such as idea fluency, originality, and diversity.[5]

In an effort to examine Idea Generation from the inside, researchers have also sought to map how creativity and new ideas unfold in our brains. One neuroscientist invited a group of freestyle rappers to perform while their brains were being scanned by fMRI machines. The results revealed how improvisational speech taps into an entirely different network of neurons from more scripted forms of expression. In a rap battle, the rhymes race out so fast there's no time for conscious thinking, only the spontaneous remixing of memories into words. Inventing on the fly, rappers draw on memories and self-control but also deeper, faster reflexes and motivations. The resulting spontaneous expression relies on the brain's breadbasket of memories, including our experiences and everything we can recall of what we've read, watched, or learned. And by selecting and combining both relevant and irrelevant memories in new ways, we innovate.[6]

Never Say No

The advertising tycoon Alex Osborn was the first person to pioneer the instantaneous sharing of possible solutions in a group setting, a process he called "brainstorming." In his 1953 book, *Applied Imagination: Principles and Procedures of Creative Thinking*, Osborn explained how this meant, quite literally, "using the *brain to storm* a creative problem—and to do so in a *commando* fashion, with each stormer audaciously attacking the same objective."[7]

One of the cardinal rules of brainstorming is "never say no," a tenet it shares with improvisational comedy. For example, if your acting partner walks onstage as a giraffe in an evening gown, you could end up as a confused seamstress taking the dress order, a monkey frantically sewing a matching suit, or possibly a zookeeper who can't find his measuring tape and scissors. Whatever happens, improvisational actors must always accept and support the creative decisions of their fellow performers. They train by saying "yes, and . . ." over and over, until it becomes a natural response.

Offstage, business leaders have embraced this technique to encourage their teams to work collaboratively and, if possible, build upon one another's ideas. You don't have to agree with everything your co-workers suggest, but the goal is to make sure no grain of creative potential goes unhulled. People who score as Brainstormers often excel in work settings where they stimulate conversation and can help produce a large volume of potential solu-

tions, feeding grain into the mill. Many companies today
see brainstorming as the key to unlocking innovation and
sustaining the competitive edge they need to survive.

The Exercise

In this exercise, you'll be asked to answer a seemingly nonsensical or
clearly ridiculous question. The prompt concerns an outlandish topic
such as "What would you do if you knew that one week from today you
would grow twenty inches taller?" Or "What would the world be like
if the wheel had never been invented?" Or "How many different ways
could you use a paperclip?" The test gives you only a few minutes to
respond, and the utter randomness of the question is key. Only someone
whose brain is inclined to gush ideas will be able to quickly orient themselves to the given scenario and unleash a flood of imaginative answers
regardless of their relevance, practicality, or adherence to convention.
By contrast, a Concentrated Focuser will approach their answer more
carefully, with greater attention to the ideas themselves. For many on
the left end of the Idea Generation continuum, the utter absurdity of the
prompt will leave them flummoxed and thinking too deeply about the
best or most literal response.

This assessment measures only the quantity of your ideas, not their
quality, creativity, or connection to the question. A Brainstormer's answers sometimes lack any consistent thread at all, branching off like twigs
in every direction. Indeed, Idea Generation and creativity are only mildly
connected, and the test is not meant to measure originality or imagination. Instead, it captures how many answers a person can pluck out of
their brain, on topics both familiar and unfamiliar, in a short span of time.

The Brainstormer

In a recent conversation with former *Top Chef* contestant and TV personality Carla Hall, we found ourselves swept onto her animated idea train, a ride that could rival that of a Disney theme park. Like many Brainstormers, Hall is warm, vivacious, and chatty, bouncing and swerving between reflections of past experiences and a roster of future plans, all while putting us at ease with her self-effacing humor.

We were surprised to learn that she graduated from Howard University with a degree in accounting, a discipline not especially conducive to Brainstormers. "I chose to major in it because I truly enjoyed the classes. But when I took a position at Price Waterhouse, I found the actual work incredibly stifling," she explained. Secure in the knowledge that her education would give her many options, Hall took a risk and followed an exciting short-term opportunity to work as a fashion model in Europe. "I was young and looking for adventure. I knew that accounting would still be there, but deep down I recognized that the profession wasn't the right place for me."

Two years later, Hall returned to the States and cobbled together a livelihood, unsure of her next move. One of her jobs was operating a small catering service that she dubbed "The Lunch Basket," which brought her some notoriety as a chef in Washington, DC. Wildly popular and somewhat accidental, this start-up led her to culinary stardom when she was offered a chance to compete on *Top Chef*. Performing on live television came easily to her, and audiences loved both her on-screen persona and her genius in the kitchen. With her natural wit and bubbly energy, she churned out ideas like a happy hen laying eggs. She was the perfect fit for the rapidly growing, unscripted world of reality television.

Hall is at her best when she simultaneously has her hands in many different pots. Having fully embraced her strengths, she now fills her days with an eclectic mix of professional and personal projects, from publishing children's books to acting to judging the National Gingerbread House Competition to serving as a nutrition consultant for high school cafeterias. She even makes time for creative hobbies (during our Zoom interview, she excitedly held up a piece of artwork made from colorful woven paper, her latest creative outlet). This woman won't sit still.

"I have several new shows starting," she told us at the time of the interview, including "a travelogue show called *Chasing Flavor*."[8] Hall is an expert at pitching diverse approaches to a project, themes for a party, or plot twists for a story. But when operating at full speed, she is prone to go off on not just tangents, but tangents of tangents. Like the Swedish inventor Simone Giertz, Hall has come to embrace a self-made career that takes full advantage of this tendency through regular variety, novelty, and unexpected turns.

Like Pat Shea, Hall also delights in extemporaneous speaking including impromptu stand-up comedy. The ability to "wing it" and shoot from the hip is part of what makes these Brainstormers so naturally engaging and magnetic.

Rolling in Ideas

Looking for a creative boost? Simone Giertz's idea dice offer one fun and satisfying solution. Armed with a delightful variety of potential combinations, they are guaranteed to generate new, creative, and often wonky suggestions with every roll (what Giertz cheekily calls "lubrication for your creative process"). As Giertz commented, "Coming up with ideas out of thin air is really hard. Having some initial parameters can help make it easier and help lower the bar. I love a bar that is so low that I can crawl over it." You might, for example, roll Vehicle, Trash, and Makes Music; or Gift, Fabric, and One-Day Build. Whether you actually bring these projects to reality is beside the point. The real goal is to challenge what is possible and push your brain's creative limits.

In a YouTube video, Giertz and her cocreator, Laura, roll their new dice and respond to the prompts Furniture, Trash, and One-Day Build. Amid a smattering of dirty jokes and hilarity, they go on to create a chair built from a discarded satellite dish in a single day. "We went with an idea that I would have never come up with or chosen," Giertz told us, adding that she loves the surprise of finding an unexpected challenge. A few months after posting the satellite chair video, she put up the shiny metal dice for sale on her website, Yetch.store, for sixty-five dollars ("Yetch" is the correct pronunciation of "Giertz" in her native Swedish). They sold out almost immediately. As it turns out, Giertz's YouTube videos are excellent marketing material. Why? Because, like most Brainstormers, she loves to chat. Indeed, we recognize this kind of energy in other famous Brainstormers, including Walt Disney, Steve Jobs, Robin Williams, and Eminem.[9]

Brainstormer Challenges

You never know when a daydream or a fun little jaunt down a rabbit hole may lead to the next big innovation. But even the most prolific minds have to occasionally commit their full concentration to a single project. When faced with repetitive activities that require intense, prolonged focus, Brainstormers lay out the welcome mat for distraction. Constrained by classroom environments, some students who need more outlets for their percolating ideas find themselves fidgeting in their seats, staring out the window, talking to their friends, or tapping their toes until the school bell rings.

Joel Savitt, director of Google Developer Studio, was one of those kids. He found school easy, but he struggled with boredom, which his grades reflected. He was constantly distracted and prone to daydreaming. He struggled to engage, and he couldn't bring himself to stick to just one area of interest. Savitt approached his enrollment at the University of Maryland, College Park, as a purely "social endeavor," because there didn't seem to be any other good reason to go. When that particular endeavor failed, he got kicked out of school. "So those were my college years, if you can call them college years," Savitt jokes, vowing to keep his college transcripts hidden from his college-bound daughters.

Savitt eventually found his way in the entertainment industry. "I was fortunate enough to land a 'lofty' position in the mailroom at the Dick Clark Productions," he recalled, but it was not the best place for his ideas to run wild. Still, he got lucky. On his second day on the job, he caught wind of an opening for a production assistant on a new show called *Will You Marry Me?* He immediately volunteered, bumping his daily earnings up to fifty dollars (from forty) and, more important, taking a first step toward the kind of work he is wired to do. Today he runs programs that he created to drive efficiency in the production of video content across Google's many divisions. In his work with worldwide creatives, no two days are the same.

Amid the tumult of layoffs and uncertainty in the tech world in late 2022 and early 2023, Savitt rode out the storm. "In those moments of ambiguity, there are things that you know," he commented. And "maybe my ability to generate lots of ideas helped me through in ways I didn't even realize. It's just sort of the way that I react or move in a certain space or time."[10]

Another common challenge for Brainstormers is filtering their thoughts. They do their best work when they find collaborators who are good at pruning, prioritizing, selecting, and implementing ideas. In Carla Hall's case, none of her copious and creative ideas would come to fruition without the right team. Hall's current assistant is a researcher and top-notch implementer who is the perfect fit. She excels at giving Hall the support she needs to make a choice and take action on her best ideas. Like a skilled lifeguard, she can be counted on to drag Hall in from the sea of possibilities to the beach of achievable reality. "We work so well together," Hall gushes. Her assistant has become both the driver and the filter behind Hall's success.[11]

If you are a Brainstormer, the mental clutter of so many ideas can feel overwhelming and cause you to feel confused or lose focus. Trying to express your thoughts as quickly as they flow can potentially turn into a bad habit of interrupting people. Journaling, regular meditation, shutting off your smartphone, and minimizing distractions from digital devices are all good strategies to help you avoid getting pulled into this idea vortex.

Brainstormers at Work

Certain types of careers will bring the greatest satisfaction and stimulation to people whose brains produce a copious, effortless flow of ideas. Jobs that provide fertile grounds for their idea abundance include corporate training, courtroom litigation, social media marketing, and songwriting to name a few. (See the Appendix for some examples of job types and other activities that align with those who score as Brainstormers.)

The Concentrated Focuser

Captain James Edward Reeves had spent almost nine thousand hours commanding the cockpit when, on an overcast Wednesday morning in September 1974, he climbed aboard a "Whisper Jet" McDonnell Douglas DC-9 loaded with seventy-eight passengers. He and copilot James Daniels kept up a steady banter about politics and used cars throughout the twenty-minute flight from Charleston, South Carolina, to Charlotte, North Carolina, where the forecast was dense fog.

After initiating their descent, Captain Reeves rattled off the plane's altitude above sea level—1,800 feet—but he confused the two cockpit altimeters. Their destination airport was located at field level—726 feet above sea level. Roaring along at almost 200 miles per hour, they were flying at an altitude 450 feet below the minimum requirement for a safe landing. No one corrected him.

"We're all ready," noted Reeves. "All we've got to do is find the airport." Seconds later, the plane slammed into a field some three miles short of the runway. The crash killed seventy-two people, including late-night TV host Stephen Colbert's father and two older brothers. Together with five other on-approach accidents around the same time, this tragedy drove the creation of a new protocol. The so-called sterile cockpit rule prohibits all cockpit conversation not relating directly to aircraft operation and safety below ten thousand feet.[12] This strict new policy became necessary because, for many of us, it takes a concerted effort to eliminate distractions.

But for the Concentrated Focuser, tunnel vision comes naturally.

A wide range of occupations require activities that place people in hazardous, high-pressure, multifaceted, and uncertain environments. These include piloting aircraft, administering anesthesia, operating drill rigs, and myriad others.[13] In many of these roles, being able to endure long hours of boredom punctuated, as one anesthesiologist put it, "by moments of sheer terror," is essential.[14]

We interviewed Dr. Chris Peterson, chair of Lancaster General Hospital's department of anesthesia. Dr. Peterson is a Concentrated Focuser. Peterson was first drawn to his profession while doing rounds in the pediatric ward during medical school. When a patient in the emergency room suddenly had a problem with their airway, "the anesthesiologist was incredibly calm even though the room seemed to be in chaos," he remembered. "Everyone had a job to perform, but I immediately felt drawn to that role. The ability to shut out distractions and focus has always come easily to me, and I immediately saw how this could be an asset to patient safety and impact many lives."

Peterson's chosen career requires a single-minded preoccupation with detail and an exceptionally high tolerance for stress. The drugs he regularly uses to anesthetize patients put them to sleep, and, in some cases, purposely arrest their breathing. He carefully monitors their vital signs, escorting them through the various phases of anesthesia.

Similar to a cockpit, the sterilized operating theater is equipped with drapes that separate the patient's head from the body. This encourages the doctor's full concentration on the surgical field. Peterson can quickly notice warning signs such as blood loss. Throughout the operation, nurses, anesthesiologists, doctors, and technicians must work in perfect harmony, with the clearest and most succinct communication possible.

While Brainstormers rely on strategies to suppress intrusive thoughts and ideas to offset their talent for Idea Generation, Concentrated Focusers' relative internal quiet gives them an advantage when seeking meditative peace. Dr. Peterson, who is also an ordained Buddhist priest, has found enormous benefits in leading weekly Zen meditation groups. "I first became interested in mindfulness and meditation as a means to reduce my level of stress," he notes. "It has made me a better doctor. As an anesthesiologist, I meet with patients prior to surgery, when their anxieties are at their height. I've found that my calm interactions with them, and in all my relationships, have improved because of my medi-tation practice."[15]

In a similarly high-stress working environment, a Brainstormer might use meditation as a means to escape their racing mind. But for Dr. Peterson and other Concentrated Focusers, it's another chance to sink happily into prolonged periods that allow them to filter out inter-ruptions and ignore everything but the most necessary stimuli.[16] For example, former air traffic controller Chris Eaton described reaching his state of quietude when immersed in the natural world. "I wouldn't say I'm much of a backpacker, per se. But I love being in national parks and historic sites," he told us. "Just being surrounded by nature's beauty, that's where I feel like I'm at home. I feel at peace."[17]

The ability to fend off distractions is highly valued in not just the operating theater but entrepreneurial settings. With their knack for im-plementing ideas and shepherding inspirations from concept to reality, Concentrated Focusers excel as business managers. They also tend to be practical—if not ruthless—when it comes to their deployment of time and resources.

Concentrated Focuser Challenges

Concentrated Focusers can find themselves getting drowned out or in-terrupted by Brainstormers and might on occasion feel like they have to "shout" just to be heard. They also dislike being compelled to weigh in on less familiar subjects, and prefer meetings that stay strictly on topic. Some Concentrated Focusers who work in an open-plan office environment need help drowning out the extraneous chatter. Wearing headphones and listening to music can help, as long as it doesn't end up isolating you, alienating co-workers, or preventing collaboration.

Unlike Brainstormers, who simply move on with more suggestions,

Concentrated Focusers can feel bruised or deflated when their ideas get dismissed or shot down because each one represents a commitment of time and careful consideration. Some Concentrated Focusers may benefit from what Wharton professor Adam Grant calls "brainwriting." As Grant notes, ideas can be lost in group settings when people bite their tongues in response to noise, potential ego threats, or the pressure to conform. He suggests having people "brainwrite" instead, or write down their ideas separately and then convene afterward to discuss, evaluate, and refine the written suggestions. As he points out, "group wisdom begins with individual creativity," and not all such creativity blooms in the same environment.[18]

Concentrated Focusers at Work

Concentrated Focusers excel in careers that value focus and follow-through, and they are most satisfied when they see a good idea come to life. For example, they make excellent salespeople and thrive when promoting a clearly defined product or service, especially when they are supported by formal resources or established guidelines. They rarely promise things they can't deliver, and they adhere closely to what is feasible and practical.

Additionally, the immersive, cognitively demanding field of computer programming also plays to the strengths of the Concentrated Focuser. Many coders report spending an hour each day just warming up, doing a quick tutorial, reviewing a completed algorithm or playing their favorite coding game in preparation to start their work.[19] Similar to a rehearsal or a breathing exercise, this practice helps them get in the zone and cue their brains for the intense concentration and mental exertions ahead. (See the Appendix for some examples of job types and other activities that align with those who score as Concentrated Focusers.)

The Idea Contributor

Idea Contributors are pragmatic refiners who can generate a healthy volume of ideas on demand, particularly if they know something about the subject matter, but they find the greatest satisfaction in roles related to nurturing and shaping an existing idea. In a brainstorming session, they gravitate toward playing traffic cop by prompting a steady flow of inputs, parking extraneous contributions, and keeping the discussion on track. Idea Contributors favor idea quality over quantity, and they easily recognize when to close the idea valve and set down to work. Their bailiwick is elaborating, editing, and developing a step-by-step plan to see an idea come to life. One friend of ours who helps develop book concepts calls herself an "idea midwife," an apt name for many Idea Contributors.

Like Brainstormers, Idea Contributors welcome new ideas but, like Concentrated Focusers, they're not easily distracted by an incessant storm of ideas. They would agree wholeheartedly with Mark Twain, who famously quipped, "There is no such thing as a new idea."[20] While this sentiment is a source of angst for those who pride themselves on originality, the cyclical rhythm of history and even the activity of our own neurons belies the fallacy of the completely original idea. Just as the brain relies heavily on memories and experiences to generate new concepts, Idea Contributors drive innovation by improving upon existing notions.[21]

Consider, for example, the Lutheran minister-in-training, Jonas Sorensen. Deep in theological texts during his final year of seminary, he read works by Martin Luther, Søren Kierkegaard, Kathryn Tanner, and Paul Tillich. Each of these thinkers built on the concepts of those who came before them, just as Sorensen is doing now. He yearns to share more accessible views on spirituality, and in his own writing, he can expand upon the ideas, theories, and teachings from the last two thousand years. "Often, when I'm reading a passage, I think to myself, 'I've read that before.' Everything I read begins to sound like a recycled version of something written a few—or a few hundred—years ago," he says.[22] He doesn't need to find ways to be excessively original. The old teachings just need a facelift.

Updating, iterating, and improving can give rise to new classics. For example, Shakespeare's *Romeo and Juliet* was developed from an earlier poem, "The Tragicall Historye of Romeus and Juliet." Likewise, the folk and blues genre has a long tradition of borrowing; Bob Dylan famously said his songs "didn't get here by themselves."[23] Both hitchhiked and improved upon the concepts of others. These thinkers don't always have their own treasure trove of original ideas waiting to be set free, but they excel at entering into a flow state with others, naturally building on someone else's initiative to come up with more. Just as a tiny spikelet of foxtail barley hitchhikes on your sock in its quest to propagate, idea hitchhikers use one idea as a vehicle to reach another. They like to start with a template and expand on it. In doing so, they craft better solutions.

As Sorensen noted, this skill is fundamental in the academic world. No journal is ever going to accept an article without a bibliography. As an Idea Contributor, a key part of illustrating your ingenuity is demonstrating the depth of your research, your knowledge of prior sources, and your confidence that your ideas differ from what came before.

Indeed, innovation that breaks too cleanly from the past, flying straight out of left field, is more likely to spark suspicion than admiration or respect. For millennia, the oral histories and cultural identities of most human societies have relied on the compounding of myths and legends over time. The power and endurance of these stories spring from their ability to gradually shift and reflect the lives of the people who share them.

Idea Contributors also make excellent facilitators, navigating easily between Brainstormers and Concentrated Focusers. Holly Fowler, a consultant for various US Environmental Protection Agency (EPA) programs, considers herself a parachutist who drops into towns that are seeking to revitalize by improving community access to outdoor recreation and leisure. When Fowler is called in for a consulting project, she starts by refining the town's shared objectives. She helps to lead brainstorming sessions to generate as many ideas as possible from a broad group of stakeholders. At community meetings, she listens closely to every conceivable idea, ranging from expanding trail networks and building sidewalks to adding more broadband, lodging, restaurants, and other attractions to downtown areas. She calls a stop when she feels there is "enough input to go to the action-planning table and put down the concrete steps the town needs to advance their goals." She describes the effect of this process as "catalytic," noting how dozens of American towns have emerged with a newfound trove of resources, shared purpose, and opportunities to attract additional funding.[24]

Blending the Brainstormer's ability to think and navigate on the fly with the Concentrated Focuser's talent for analysis and execution, Fowler thrives in this role. Like a captain deftly steering a ship, she harnesses her positive, infectious enthusiasm to gather ideas, guide discussions, identify the best possible solutions, and set a course for how to get there.

Idea Contributor Challenges

One of the greatest challenges for Idea Contributors is striking a balance between developing existing ideas and allowing their own inspirations to flow. They also shouldn't be surprised if they occasionally experience brainstorming fatigue, especially when they can "take or leave" the topic. While Idea Contributors excel at invigorating a brainstorming session when the subject matter interests them, their ideas can dry up when it doesn't. They add real value to a team by keeping people on track and getting things done, but they can feel frustrated working on projects that are ill defined or if the direction keeps changing. "Mission creep," a challenge common among nonprofit organizations, causes acute irritation to the Idea Contributor who is adept at staying the course.

Striking a balance between contributing to the creation of worthwhile projects and bringing said projects to fruition is key for those with this aptitude. The freedom to experiment and try a new perspective on an old concept can be particularly vital, but not every job offers that kind of flexibility. If, on the other hand, you feel overwhelmed by the breadth of possible ways you could apply this aptitude both in and outside the workplace, take a closer look at your interests profile, work approach, and personality style. Doing so can help you narrow your focus, select the most promising ideas, and find the greatest fulfillment.

Idea Contributors at Work

If you are lucky enough to be an Idea Contributor, a wide array of career possibilities will suit your unique capacity to generate and hone ideas. While you might thrive in careers that reward rapid Idea Generation, you will also be content in jobs where the emphasis is a balance between originating new ideas and implementing existing concepts, such as curriculum development, occupational therapy, and systems analysis. (See the Appendix for some examples of job types and other activities that align with those who score as Idea Contributors.)

Unlocking a Dynamic New World

Recent advances in artificial intelligence (AI) are starting to challenge what we know about Idea Generation. Generative AI refers to a computer's ability to produce original text, creative writing, blog posts, artwork, and programming code. In these processes, a computer builds its knowledge and creates new information based on past experience and massive stores of data gathered from the internet. However, at the time of this writing, generative AI still needs a human to enter a prompt and then check the resulting answer for accuracy. Still, this bleeding-edge innovation is causing a stir.[25]

Like it or not, technologies such as ChatGPT have revolutionized how we create and communicate. Whereas Simone Giertz's idea dice offer an analog solution to spurring creative thought, all generative AI needs to suggest near-infinite possibilities is a single-word prompt. As Wharton School of Business professor Ethan Mollick has quipped, "the thing people come away with if they play with ChatGPT for just a few minutes is, wow, I can cheat on essays with this thing. And then if they spend a couple more minutes, they say, well, I can cheat on creating software code or translating language." He recommends approaching the software with caution, as if "you are chatting with an omniscient, eager-to-please intern who sometimes lies to you."[26]

Generative AI is already being used in various forms of marketing, advertising, toy design, and knowledge management. Microsoft is rolling it out in Word, Paint, and other programs to support greater creativity.[27] In academia, doctors and professors are using ChatGPT to write recommendation letters. Mollick calls it a "multiplier of ability" that holds enormous potential for maximizing human achievement. But he also cautions that the ethical implications are massive, and this kind of technology could eventually "replace all of us." Knowing where you stand on the Idea Generation continuum can help you understand how you might best use this new technology, or whether you should take a prospective job that relies heavily on it. A Brainstormer might find it stifling, for example, while a Concentrated Focuser could benefit from occasional use.

You now understand that the amount of satisfaction you draw from generating original ideas varies from person to person, and whether a machine can do it for you or not doesn't change your innate abilities. Your aptitudes simply cannot be powered down.

CHAPTER 5

Inductive Reasoning

*There are known knowns—there are things we know that we know.
We also know there are known unknowns—that is to say, we know
there are some things we do not know. But there are also unknown
unknowns, the ones we don't know we don't know.*

—Donald Rumsfeld

INDUCTIVE REASONING

Fact Checker	⟨ ⟨ ⟨ ⟨ ⟨	Investigator	⟩ ⟩ ⟩ ⟩ ⟩	Diagnostic Problem Solver

Shortly after midnight on September 26, 1983, the world came aston-
ishingly close to Armageddon. We owe our survival largely to the quick
thinking and Inductive Reasoning of a single man who just happened
to be in charge of the world's fate that night.

Soviet Air Defense Lieutenant Colonel Stanislav Petrov had one job: to
monitor the Soviet satellite system for any signs of a US attack. As usual,
the skies over the USSR had been quiet. But then suddenly the word
LAUNCH flashed in large, bright red letters across his computer screen.[1]

The brand-new ballistic missile early warning system, a system Petrov had personally helped to build, indicated with "high reliability" that American forces had just unleashed an intercontinental ballistic missile (ICBM) in the direction of the Soviet Union.[2]

Soviet protocol for this scenario dictated that, on seeing the alarm, Petrov should immediately hit the red start button. He and everyone else on duty that night knew his action would trigger a cascade of lightning-fast, automatic reactions. In the total absence of any further human input, a full-scale nuclear counterstrike would unfold, and millions would die.[3] A shocked silence gripped the room as everyone waited to see what Petrov would do.

Then another missile warning popped up, followed by another, and then another. In rapid succession, the computer reported five separate, and identical, launch alarms about an incoming missile from the United States.

Still staring at the screen, Petrov's mind raced. Of course, such an attack was a distinct possibility. The long-standing Cold War tensions between the United States and the USSR had recently escalated after Soviet missiles shot down Korean Air Lines Flight 007, killing all 269 people aboard. So far, the United States had rejected the idea that Soviet forces had mistaken the passenger plane for a spy. Suddenly, the killing of millions of civilians around the world seemed more possible.[4]

At that moment, Petrov's gift unfurled itself.

"I just couldn't believe that just like that, all of a sudden, someone would hurl five missiles at us," Petrov said. "Five missiles wouldn't wipe us out. The United States had not five, but a thousand missiles in battle readiness." Why would they use only five? It didn't make logical sense.[5]

Having helped to design the new detection system himself, Petrov was all too aware of potential errors. How had each of the warnings passed so rapidly through the thirty layers of verification they'd carefully installed?[6] By the time the last warning appeared, the ground radar should have already spotted the first incoming missiles crossing the horizon. Why, he wondered, had nothing been reported? Still, he was required to respond immediately, in the moment.

Instinct held him back. "I had a funny feeling in my gut," Petrov said later.[7]

Petrov himself was in danger. What might it mean to break military protocol? He and everyone in that room had grown up with rumors of disappeared relatives and Siberian work camps. He knew he would pay dearly for disobeying an order. But if obedience meant causing World War III and nuclear holocaust, Petrov already knew he could never stand that responsibility.

"At that moment, there was no time to think; I had to work, work, work," he remembered.[8] Less than a minute after receiving the last alarm, Petrov made his decision. He notified his supervisors of an error message. Then they all waited. If Petrov was mistaken, multiple nuclear missiles would strike the Soviet Union in the next half hour. They never did.

Later analyses revealed that the early warning system did, indeed, contain a number of bugs. The error that almost caused a nuclear war was triggered by a satellite malfunction.[9]

Like an emergency room doctor diagnosing a mysteriously ill patient, Petrov relied on just a few discrete clues to reach a critical decision under incredible time pressure. And in using his Inductive Reasoning to make the right call at that moment, he saved us all from a global catastrophe.

Going with Your Gut

Johnson O'Connor described Inductive Reasoning as "the ability to sense a unifying principle running through miscellany."[10] It is the bridge that leads us from isolated observations to the broader patterns that offer a much-needed dose of order and predictability to our lives. Like a mental funnel, Inductive Reasoning suggests a response by narrowing the available information into a single, clear thread. The resulting solution may not be the "right" one or the only one, and in many cases, it is neither. But it's fast, and it *feels* right. Often, it's not too far off the mark. And in Petrov's case, it saved millions of lives.

The idea for the Inductive Reasoning exercise stems from a nonverbal intelligence test published in 1921 by Caroline E. and Harry C. Myers. A decade later, the Johnson O'Connor Research Foundation developed it further, making it more consistent and reliable. They observed that both lawyers and physicians were particularly adept at the exercise, prompting them to call this the "Diagnostic" aptitude.

The Exercise

In this exercise you'll be asked to identify a common element among three out of six images.

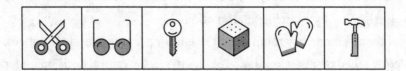

These pictures flash onto the screen rapidly and for only a few seconds, so the connections among new sets will become increasingly ambiguous.

With ample time, most people can correctly sort and classify the objects according to the same patterns, but people like Petrov in the story above do so almost instantly.[11]

Diagnostic Problem Solvers, including Petrov, tend to feel comfortable making assumptions and standing by them, even in the face of uncertainty. Deadlines motivate them, and even with limited information at hand, they trust their instincts. As Chris Karlsmose, a Denmark-based consultant at Bain & Company, confessed: "I am much more productive when there's a deadline coming. I try not to put off things until the last moment, or unnecessarily procrastinate, but having a looming time crunch definitely helps."[12] At the other end of the continuum, Fact Checkers find the pressure to give a rapid response stressful. Regardless of whether or not their answer is correct, they frequently second-guess themselves or wish for more time in order to feel confident in their decision.

Diagnostic Problem Solvers use Inductive Reasoning to rapidly identify connections between new, disparate, or disorganized pieces of information, spot inconspicuous patterns, and make likely inferences from a short list of squishy facts. When presented with new information that contradicts a prior conclusion, they are malleable and willing to reevaluate. Scientists rely on Inductive Reasoning to form new hypotheses as evidence continues to emerge. Life insurance underwriters deploy it when setting premiums based on a person's mortality risk, and poker players draw on it to calculate their odds of winning or losing a game. Neuroscientists reviewing brain scans use it to pick out the patterns in how neurological processes typically work.[13] If you enjoy crossword puzzles, firing off film critiques from the sofa, or landing quickly on the best wine in a tasting flight, you likely draw inferences with ease. Even based on very little research, you are comfortable making judgments or giving your best guess.

Confounding Sherlock?

While induction cinches a net made from empirical evidence to capture the truth, deduction lowers a small box, a preformulated hypothesis, and uses testing and fact-gathering to prove whether the truth is inside. In other words, Inductive Reasoners make sense of the world by turning specific observations into general theories, while deductive thinkers start with the theory and then test it by collecting evidence.

Sherlock Holmes has frequently been labeled a deductive thinker, but in fact he and many other famous detectives are Inductive Reasoners.[14] Starting with hard evidence, Holmes uses empirical facts to form his hypotheses. At the sight of a faint scratch on Watson's shoe or the slightest hint of cinnamon in the air, disparate connections burst like lightning across his brain. With astonishing speed, and based on just a few tiny scraps of information, he delights his readers by arriving at what is, most often, a correct conclusion (he also happens to be a Diagnostic Problem Solver).

The Diagnostic Problem Solver

As a pulmonologist at Hubei Provincial Hospital in Wuhan, China, fifty-three-year-old Dr. Zhang Jixian regularly saw patients with pneumonia-like symptoms. But on that particular Thursday in late December, an unsettling coincidence occurred. An elderly couple from a nearby residential community came in the same day with identical fever and cough symptoms. An experienced doctor, Zhang immediately recognized the rarity of encountering two family members who caught the exact same disease at the same time. And looking over the couple's CT images, she noticed something else. Both cases showed the same unusual abnormalities.[15] A haze of pale blobs clung to their lungs, partially obscuring the structures beneath. It was unlike anything she'd ever seen.

Unfazed by the novelty of the situation, Dr. Zhang's diagnostic skills churned as she rapidly pulled together disparate pieces of information, from the first cases of SARS in Foshan, China, in 2003 to her subsequent trainings in infectious disease and outbreak management. She knew exactly what to do.

Placing a call to radiology, Dr. Zhang ordered an immediate CT scan of the couple's son. His lungs showed the same abnormalities as those of his parents, and she knew then that it was serious. The next day, December 27, 2019, Dr. Zhang filed a report with her supervisors describing the family with the mysterious pneumonia symptoms. She also took steps to isolate these three patients in their own section of the hospital ward. As more patients with similar symptoms poured in over subsequent days, Dr. Zhang expanded this isolation unit to nine beds. She bought thirty pieces of protective clothing and pressed her colleagues to take precautions. Long before anyone else, she recognized Covid-19 as an emerging crisis.[16]

With their knack for instantly spotting patterns, matching personality types, and identifying potential obstacles, Diagnostic Problem Solvers like Zhang can seem clairvoyant. Nadine Cipriani, the EY executive we met earlier, provides professional services such as technology systems implementation and cybersecurity consulting to US civilian agencies. With each project proposal, she and her EY team interview potential collaborators, and "at first, everyone is dancing with everyone," she says. "But you need to come up with a compelling reason for them to join the team." In some cases, another consultant may ask to meet with EY about a partnership, but what they are really seeking is intelligence about the company's bidding strategy. It's up to Cipriani to predict their next move. "I'm always listening for clues or drawing on my past experience to determine their motivation," she says. And as her co-workers attest, her skill is uncanny.

As a Diagnostic Problem Solver, Cipriani is comfortable trusting her instincts. "It's difficult to explain, and not necessarily logical. There are a lot of data points firing all at once. Sometimes I have a hard time explaining my decisions about who to go with to my colleagues. With only a few months to complete a proposal, I have to go with my gut." And making the right choice, she says, always depends on having good data even though "I'll be honest, minutiae and detail are not my forte." This is where Fact Checkers come in. "I learned early on that it is best to rely on others for all of the fact-finding and detail," Cipriani explains.

Cipriani's reputation as a problem solver has led other EY leaders to seek her advice when facing similar problems. "They call me up and give me a set of facts. I'll ask as many questions as I can, and make a recommendation. I get a charge out of helping them reach a decision."[17] Like a law student distilling the fact pattern for a specific case down to the most poignant legal details, Cipriani mobilizes her Inductive Reasoning to quickly identify the most promising solution.

Olivia Mason, the London-based sommelier, is another Diagnostic Problem Solver who uses her unique inductive skills to critique fine wines. In 2022, she was invited to serve as a judge for the much-anticipated Decanter World Wine Awards, a privilege granted to only 250 wine experts from around the world. Each judge is invited (no, you cannot apply) based on their seasoned and discriminative knowledge of regional wines. Over 18,000 wines compete for the top fifty awards, a coveted honor. In a single sip, judges like Mason can detect the subtleties of each sample, mentally weighing them against one another and against the strict, highly specific regional standards of quality.

For many of us, simply contemplating this level of discernment is bewildering. But especially given the finite number of wines and the concrete time limit for determining a winner, Mason is in her element. She swirls, sniffs, and tastes from nine in the morning to five o'clock in the evening, passing judgment on more than 120 wines per day.

Settling on the best wine in any one category also requires sharing and collaborating with other judges in a section, forcing Mason to feel absolute certainty about her conclusions before stating them. She finds additional satisfaction in sharing her convictions and competition results through writing reviews. As she explained, "I enjoy being able to help" wine producers promote their best wines "because they've done well."[18] Part of Mason's enthusiasm for this work also comes from the knowledge that next year's entries will shuffle the rankings once more, giving her a fresh opportunity to test her Inductive Reasoning skills.

Diagnostic Problem Solver Challenges

As with any aptitude, Inductive Reasoning can induce joy or stress, depending on the situation. People who score at the right-hand end of this particular aptitude are predisposed to challenges others may not encounter as frequently, but with the right tools, these hurdles are manageable.

One of the most problematic yet beneficial traits common to Diagnostic Problem Solvers is their restlessness. In today's rapidly moving world, a love of perpetual motion can be an undisputed boon. But for Diagnostic Problem Solvers, the *lack* of a problem or the need to pivot can also become an issue. Without a steady flow of inferences to draw or puzzles to solve, boredom can set in. Many Diagnostic Problem Solvers may be driven to manufacturing crises or whipping up a needless feeling of urgency just to feel that rush of resolving a pressing issue, to the detriment of solutions and their relationships with co-workers, or family and friends.

As a Diagnostic Problem Solver, Betsy has had some memorable lessons in this regard. Figuring out the logistics of even the shortest vacations used to make her cringe because her husband, Ridley, makes decisions quite differently from the way she does. He will happily spend entire evenings trolling the internet searching for the perfect hotel or the best place to stop for lunch, and by the time they finally embark on a trip, he's left little space for serendipity.

Once, when planning a trip to Italy and France for their fifteenth wedding anniversary, she pleaded with him to let her handle just one small portion of the itinerary. He reluctantly agreed to let her arrange a two-night stay in Paris. A quick internet search yielded a travel blog that recommended two small boutique hotels in the Bonne-Nouvelle quartier, a few short blocks from the famous Jardin des Tuileries and the Louvre. The first place was too expensive but the second one, described as "eclectic and charming," met all of their criteria. With confidence and a bit of smug satisfaction at her efficiency, she reserved the room.

A few months later, after an idyllic stay at a beautiful pensione in the Italian coastal town of Portofino (the wonderful dividend of Ridley's meticulous research), they arrived in Paris. A faint smell of stale urine greeted them when they stepped into the tired little hotel she'd booked. The proprietor's ungroomed dog sauntered up to their luggage with the same shifty gaze some canines use when sizing up a fire hydrant. They followed the bedraggled owner and dog up four flights of threadbare carpeted stairs. Once the door to their "suite" was safely closed, Ridley turned to Betsy. "What, exactly, did you read about this place?" he asked.

She reached into her bag and pulled out the article she'd printed and saved. Only then did she notice her mistake: it was over ten years old.

Fortunately, Ridley had looked up an alternative Paris hotel "just in case," and they relocated that same day.

At this and other points in Betsy's life, she's had to learn the hard way about the strengths and weaknesses of her Inductive Reasoning aptitude. Among other things, she's learned that not every problem calls for Diagnostic Problem-Solving, and that having a partner who spends more time investigating the details can be a lifesaver.

Another challenge for Diagnostic Problem Solvers relates to their penchant for criticism. While the ability to cut to the root of an issue or sift through the nonsense makes them superb judges, a too-sharp tongue can backfire and sting peers, colleagues, family, or friends. Slipping into heavy critiques of yourself and your ideas is also a danger that can lead to negative spirals of self-questioning and devil's-advocate scenarios.

Then there are the times when settling quickly on a decision and sticking with it can lead to hazardous pitfalls. For example, in the absence of reliable information, Diagnostic Problem Solvers can easily fall victim to seeing connections where none exist. Moreover, the appeal of fantastical explanations increases when we feel gripped by crisis (a trend that helps drive conspiracy theories). In an era of AI-generated deep fakes, Diagnostic Problem Solvers need to be especially vigilant with regards to the quality of the information they consume. At its worst, as psychologist Karen Douglas notes, when we are stressed or pressured our brains are programmed to rapidly find order and "to simplify and name things that may be too nuanced for us to understand."[19] It's the perfect scenario for the birth and spread of stereotypes. Still, as long as Diagnostic Problem Solvers remain open to factual information, they are quick to alter their hypotheses accordingly.

Regardless of where you fall on the Inductive Reasoning continuum, your ability to spot patterns and connections will accelerate as your knowledge and expertise in a given area increases. Thus, even if all emergency room physicians aren't Diagnostic Problem Solvers, their years of medical training allow them to rapidly recognize and respond when a patient shows symptoms of a stroke. That said, being a diagnostic physician will not necessarily mean you are good at reading the healthcare stock market.

If you are a right-end scorer in Inductive Reasoning, you will find your best and most fulfilling work by combining this aptitude with expertise, practice, and training. Cultivating particular expertise in this way can also position you to share your gift of discernment in contexts where it will be most constructive and valued.

Diagnostic Problem Solvers at Work

Diagnostic Problem Solvers are most likely to find satisfaction in work that engages their ability to critique and advise, draw conclusions, or come up with solutions. They also enjoy challenges that require zeroing in on the root of a pressing issue. These natural sleuths can sniff out solutions for challenging problems, whether it's finding the answer to a vexing archaeological mystery or simply identifying the cause of an annoying "check engine" light. (See the Appendix for some examples of job types and other activities that align with those who score as Diagnostic Problem Solvers.)

The Fact Checker

"Can I get a bit more information?" or "Would it be okay if we sleep on this?" are both common requests made by Fact Checkers or those who inhabit the left end of the Inductive Reasoning continuum. Rather than relying on Inductive Reasoning, these meticulous minds take a thorough and methodical approach to problem-solving. Patient information gatherers, they prefer a job that allows them plenty of time to deliberate before drawing a conclusion. They value accuracy above all, and they dislike being pushed to act prematurely by, for example, an artificial deadline.

Fact Checkers do their best work when they have enough data and time to form a carefully considered opinion. This thoughtful approach leads to great precision, a trait treasured by colleagues, employers, and partners. Just as the world needs Diagnostic Problem Solvers to offer aid in an emergency, Fact Checkers are needed to determine what is and is not verifiable truth. These left-end scorers play a crucial role in keeping our society healthy, safe, and functioning smoothly.

Today's instantaneous communications and 24-7 social connectivity have made the calm, calculated pace so fundamental to the work of Fact Checkers a rarity, leaving us exposed to con artists, swindlers, and liars. Take the case of George Santos, the former Republican representative from New York who admitted to lying about his work experience and education before he was elected in November 2022. During his campaign, he falsely claimed to have earned a degree from Baruch College and held jobs at Citigroup and Goldman Sachs, among other things. While Democratic opposition researchers hunted down some contradictory evidence relating to a few of his bigger claims, they failed to "kick the tires" on the most basic ones. And so, he won a seat in Congress.

A Fact Checker could have easily found evidence to prove or disprove Santos's claims by searching education databases and old yearbooks, or just asking around nicely. As any good researcher can attest, digging into even the most mundane details can reveal a very different picture from what at first appears obvious. The finest details are the very ones that often expose the full and necessary truth.

Carrington Fox used to make a living digging for truths like these. A Princeton graduate, she got an MBA from Vanderbilt in 2001 and landed a job reporting on business for *The Tennessean*, a daily news-paper. While writing quick 700- or 1,000-word pieces on a variety of topics indulged her insatiable curiosity, the tight deadlines worked against her Fact Checker instincts. "In responsible journalism, every-thing needs to come from a credible source," she explained. "There's no winging it." She remembers a lot of rigorous editing. "I spent as much time confirming material as I did composing it."

Fox's favorite work was developing feature stories for a monthly mag-azine that allowed her to take more time, dive deep into details, and do plenty of fact-checking. In writing about cooking, she found she "loved going down rabbit holes to learn about ingredients. You'd be surprised how much there is to know about foie gras, hops, or seasonal pastries!"

After more than two decades of writing and raising children, Fox switched careers and took up home construction. It all started with her first home purchase and the jarring realization that she had no idea how to actually take care of a house, never mind how to unclog a drain. She felt uneasy considering her options to renovate without first learning all there was to know about home repair, from fixing a broken toilet to patching a leaky roof. So, she enrolled in a course about rehabilitating buildings at the local technical college. She went on to earn her degree in building and construction from the Tennessee College of Applied Technology and, while she was at it, documented each hands-on expe-rience on her personal blog, *Build Me Up, Buttercup*.[20]

In her current work for a renovation and maintenance company, Fox still sees many parallels with journalism. "Identifying the source of a leak can require some digging, and not just figuratively," she noted. "Many problems we encounter in construction also have more than one solution. I'm hardwired to consider all of them." For example, replacing a rotten deck can prompt a series of inquiries: Which brand of compos-ite wood has the top Consumer Reports rating? Is this supplier offering the best price? Do the subcontractors provide a warranty when installing this product? "I know it sounds geeky, but finding the source for a piece of vintage millwork or a specific doorknob to match an existing style throughout a home gives me a charge," Fox said.[21]

Scenario planning and disaster preparedness come easily to Fact Checkers, making them valued members of any special event team. They can channel their distaste for split-second decisions into creating elaborate drills that anticipate all types of surprises from weather events to bomb threats. This may include devising strategies to ensure that even the most ambiguous or uncertain situation has been rehearsed. These hyper-preparers draw satisfaction from the knowledge that their layers of backup plans (which, also have backup plans!) are in place to ensure a seamless response to any calamity.

Fact-Checker Challenges

If you are a Fact Checker, you thrive in work that allows you to use or build a structured environment for solving problems. You may become anxious or stressed by work that requires rapid decisions, especially over the long term. If you feel uneasy about having to come up with a quick answer to a complex issue, you might want to consider asking for a deadline extension. The anxiety associated with this situation also eases with experience. When she first started working in construction management, Fox's boss told her that, though he appreciated her thoroughness, she was taking too long to work up the bids for services. As it turned out Fox just needed a little more time on the job to learn how to discern between a novel and a routine repair project. "There are always new products to explore and new styles to choose from in the building industry," she explained, and so "I have to be sure perfection isn't the enemy of the good."[22]

Though Fact Checkers can spot patterns comfortably and easily when a subject is familiar, they can struggle when time is tight and they cannot turn to others for help in identifying or validating patterns. Without enough time to properly cross the *t*s and dot the *i*s, these thinkers end up feeling less satisfied because they believe the outcome could have been better or more certain. If this situation applies to you, it can help to try to manage your expectations in advance and remind yourself that nothing is perfect. The world runs on best efforts. When tackling new tasks, Fact Checkers are likely to ask for further explanation or more examples than most people. Colleagues or partners who highlight distinct pros and cons can help these meticulous minds land on a decision more efficiently.

Fact Checkers at Work

A number of professions rely on careful deliberators. For example, a good hiring manager will thoroughly evaluate candidates by collecting input from several stakeholders, then following up by conducting careful background checks. Risk officers, pharmacists, travel agents, data scientists, computer programmers, attorneys, and accountants all have to constantly check and recheck their data, a habit that comes naturally to those who love being meticulous.

Most Fact Checkers are less suited to work that involves rapid changes and on-the-fly problem-solving, but they are often willing to stick with a job until they become comfortable, or even expert, at what they do. This patience in pursuing a goal can make them good managers, executives, or other team leaders. Work that occurs in a relatively stable, organized, and predictable environment with well-defined problem-solving parameters is ideal for this type of thinker. When given enough time to find, sift through, and process available facts and patiently support the work of others, Fact Checkers thrive. (See the Appendix for some examples of job types and other activities that align with those who score as Fact Checkers.)

The Investigator

Investigators have a strong sense of pacing. They excel at keeping a team moving efficiently, either by slowing down or speeding up collaborative decision-making. They prefer to have more information, and are more cautious, questioning, and deliberative, than Diagnostic Problem Solvers. Yet they also know when to stop scrutinizing and make a decision. Particularly when working with Fact Checkers, they have a knack for fostering action.

In an organizational setting, Investigators can drive critical decisions that are both fast and accurate, a valuable asset in large companies.[23] In his 2016 letter to shareholders, Amazon founder Jeff Bezos described his own rules for "high quality, high-velocity decision making." He argues that "most decisions should probably be made with somewhere around 70 percent of the information you *wish* you had. If you wait for 90 percent, in most cases, you're probably being slow. If you're good at course correcting, being wrong may be less costly than you think, whereas being slow is going to be expensive."[24]

Investigators can strike that essential balance between Diagnostic Problem Solvers and Fact Checkers, making them excellent team leaders. As natural pacesetters, they are comfortable casting the pivotal vote in a room full of tentative decision-makers or pressing pause when a conclusion feels too rushed. Investigators are also good at keeping themselves on pace, which makes them well suited to work as independent contractors.

If you score as an Investigator, take care to choose a working environment that aligns with your decision-making pace. For example, Investigator and Chef Sara Quessenberry does her best work when she has time to connect ideas, concepts, and past experiences before taking action. When she sold her Lake Tahoe restaurant and moved to New York City, she accepted a job in the test kitchen at *Real Simple* magazine, where she found some of the autonomy she'd enjoyed as a restaurant owner but with the bonus of a less frenetic environment. She had ample time to experiment with new recipes but also had to work within the deadlines imposed by the monthly print schedule. After the relentless pace of running a restaurant kitchen, the longer time horizon of magazine publishing felt like a luxury.

Like other Investigators, Quessenberry enjoys incorporating new information to inform her choices, and she eagerly solicits input from others. She relishes the opportunity to weave each new fact into her work, making incremental improvements even as she guards against unnecessary delays. When Jessica Seinfeld (Jerry's wife) recruited her to help write a cookbook, *Vegan at Times*, Quessenberry immediately fell in love with the work, which required both careful pacing and well-established parameters.[25] She had the task of choosing recipes, stylists, photographers, setting, aesthetic, and the overall time line for the book. It was the perfect environment for someone with her strengths.

Investigator Challenges

One of the opportunities Sarah Quessenberry explored after moving to New York was a coveted position at her "dream" culinary publication, *Gourmet* magazine. She applied for the job, and the preinterview went smoothly. But then came the cooking challenge. "The assignment was to create a main course, write a recipe for it, and cook it in one of their test kitchens," she remembers.

For an Investigator like Quessenberry, this free-form assignment without any boundaries was a bit daunting. She had to create something entirely new, and fast. "I finally settled on some chicken dish with ramps, I think. I wasn't totally confident in the dish going in, but I was confident in my skills," she says. But when she arrived for the interview, they popped a surprise. She would also have to prepare a recipe given to her on the spot, a genoise or French sponge cake with its own special "foaming method." Making a satisfactory genoise is all about chemistry, and that day her whipped sugar and eggs didn't reach quite the right consistency. She fought butterflies as she removed the cake from the oven, only to see it collapse to an embarrassingly thin three quarters of an inch.[26]

Like other Investigators, Quessenberry does her best work when she has enough space and time to set what she feels is the right working pace. Without this leverage, Investigators can become uncomfortable, stressed, or frustrated. They can stumble into mistakes, such as the genoise, that belie their years of training and expertise.

Investigators can become frustrated and feel powerless to help when they observe others engaging in hasty leaps of faith or foot-dragging, and it can be difficult to play the middleman between Diagnostic Problem Solvers and Fact Checkers. Meanwhile, building the credibility to play this role and lead a project is not something you can pick up overnight. It requires a deep knowledge base and years of patience, experience, and diligent practice.

Investigators at Work

Investigators are well suited to a broad variety of jobs that engage both diagnostic thinking and fact-checking skills. They are unlikely to become stalled by a lack of information, but when making decisions they also prefer to have ample data and adequate time. In a group setting, their teammates can count on them to set the pace and keep things moving forward. This makes them well suited for all types of project management, but also many other pursuits as broad ranging as horticulture and human resource management. (See the Appendix for some examples of job types and other activities that align with those who score as Investigators.)

Robot Reasoning

Like a mental funnel, our Inductive Reasoning points us to answers by narrowing the available information into a single, comprehensible stream. The resulting solution may not be the "right" or the only one, but it's fast and it "feels" right based on what we know. For humans, this ability to see patterns and connections only improves as we build our knowledge and experience in a particular area. But can the same ever be true for computers? Will robots ever develop "gut" feelings about things?

Whereas computers mastered deductive reasoning early on, Inductive Reasoning has posed more of a challenge. The advent of big data and digital neural networks has made it possible for today's more powerful computers to move from massive stores of relevant facts to the most logical conclusion through pattern recognition and reasoning, much as humans do.[27] With the help of machine learning, so-called computer brains are capable of learning from their own "data experiences" in a process known as cognitive computing. This ability has revolutionized artificial intelligence, starting with IBM's Watson, a machine that publicly beat two human contestants on *Jeopardy!* in 2011.[28] Since then, chat bots and other forms of artificial intelligence have become experts at "thinking" like humans.

Still, even the smartest computers continue to struggle when the rules surrounding what constitutes relevant data are hazy.[29] Unlike artificial intelligence, our human brains deftly blend Inductive Reasoning with the ability to grasp the big picture, or mentally organize large amounts of information into a logical order; an aptitude known as Sequential Reasoning.

CHAPTER 6

Sequential Reasoning

For the first 25 years of my life, I wanted freedom. For the next 25 years, I wanted order. For the next 25 years, I realized that order is freedom.

—Winston Churchill

SEQUENTIAL REASONING

Process Supporter	⟨ ⟨ ⟨ ⟨ ⟨	Collaborative Planner	⟩ ⟩ ⟩ ⟩ ⟩	Sequential Thinker

In April 2022, dozens of Yeti sightings were reported along Alaska's Gulf Coast. But this particular hubbub was not caused by the apelike creature of Himalayan lore. Rather, nearby residents described scores of bright orange, yellow, and blue coolers bobbing in the water and washing up on beaches. The source of these Yetis was the merchant vessel *Zim Kingston*, which lost some of its Yeti company cargo while weathering choppy waters outside the Port of Vancouver. Some 1,600 trendy Yeti ice chests, worth as much as $800 each, fell overboard. For months afterward, they washed ashore on beaches from Alaska and Washington State to Hawaii.[1]

The world's oceans are a bustling thoroughfare of freighters carrying millions of shipping containers that measure twenty to forty feet long. Each year, hundreds of these giant metal boxes, together with their contents, are lost at sea. A single accident in 2013 resulted in 4,293 lost containers.[2] In another highly publicized case from 2022, a ship carrying hundreds of Porsches, Bentleys, and Lamborghinis from Germany to the United States caught fire and sank, after burning for weeks.[3] Even if your new car doesn't end up at the bottom of the sea en route to your local dealership, much can go wrong between ports of call: foul weather, loading and unloading delays, lengthy maintenance inspections, and even pirate attacks.

Being able to avoid calamity under these circumstances requires diligent and highly detailed logistics planning, says merchant marine ship captain Ben Day. "My whole job is to get the ship from point A to point B," he says. "When you have a detailed plan, there are fewer fires to put out." Day's job forces him to constantly think three steps—or three ports—ahead, a skill made easier by his natural aptitude for Sequential Reasoning. Where the weight of planning and overseeing enormous and potentially dangerous seagoing operations might paralyze many, Day relishes the challenge.

The freighters he captains are like massive construction sites, and Day is the foreman. His voyages aren't just about loading a ship in Tacoma and unloading it in Okinawa; there can often be four or five stops in between. A domino effect of costly delays and narrow escapes is bound to occur without serious forethought regarding how to sequence the cargo being loaded in and out. (On one occasion, Day and his crew spent hours frantically rearranging cargo after a crane operator mistakenly deposited a container full of ammunition next to one holding flammable liquid.) When he's at sea, Day welcomes the boring days. Those are the good days, he says, because they confirm that he and his crew have done a good job of planning.

Day's crew likes to call him "Captain Flip-Flops"; instead of wearing many different hats, he wears a lot of flip-flops. Each time a vessel docks an entire team of experts, from inspectors to welders, electricians, and mechanics, set to work. As captain, Day oversees not only his own crew but each of these specialists. "I need to know how to do all of the jobs," he says.[4] Everyone connected to the ship relies on Day's leadership in their approach to their duties, their emotions, their relationships, and, most important, their safety on an unpredictable sea. Along with all the logistics, these factors are always on his mind.

Order Out of Chaos

Sequential Reasoning is the ability to solve problems by creating rational, logically ordered sequences in one's head. Also known as analytical thinking or concept organization, it determines how fast or reflexively a person mentally structures large amounts of information, often while continuing to talk, listen, or otherwise engage with the world around them.

This aptitude was identified in the 1930s when a scientist working at Johnson O'Connor's Human Engineering Laboratory stumbled on something unexpected. Tasked with creating a new measure for Inductive Reasoning, Samuel P. Horton devised a test based on words rather than images. Test takers looked at an empty diagram and a list of words, then populated the template in a logical sequence. After running the new items on a sample of test takers, Horton compared the results against the existing, picture-based Inductive Reasoning test. He found, to his surprise, that the scores did not correlate. What, then, was being measured by the words-based assessment? Further testing and analysis revealed that instead of illustrating our skill in grasping the connections between disparate things, this measure gauges the ability to arrange things quickly into a logical mental sequence.[5]

The Exercise

In this exercise, you'll be asked to arrange a set of words into a logical pattern similar to working a complex puzzle.

Use your mouse to drag and drop the words into the diagram. If you want to change an arrangement, double-clicking any tile will remove it from the diagram.

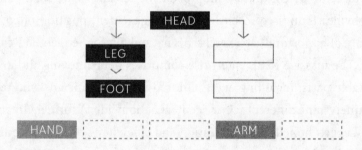

Racing to fit each word into its box, some feel a rush of satisfaction when they see the correct arrangement click into place. It just feels and looks right. Sequential Thinkers in particular enjoy this game, reveling in the opportunity to repeatedly seize upon the overarching system and order things accordingly.

Horton found that scientists, engineers, and editors all shared similar scores on this test, pointing to their shared knack for mentally sifting through, sorting, and organizing the most pertinent information to arrive at the best solutions. These master minders love thinking out loud and use analysis and logic to solve problems. Natural strategists, they can quickly and accurately pick out what's broken or absent from a system and map a path forward. They especially enjoy setting long-term goals, strategizing process improvements, prioritizing skills, and collaborating in pursuit of a shared objective. They articulate their solutions in broad strokes, identifying the big picture, then collaborate with others who help to hammer out the more detailed components. As Sequential Thinker and former US Chief Data Scientist D. J. Patil explained, "When I'm preparing a speech, I'm not thinking about the outline and then writing it. I'm spending all of my time on the message."[6]

The Sequential Thinker

As director of continuous improvement for the ICEE Company in Nashville, Tennessee, Zach Leggett's management position offers him plenty of opportunity to exercise his natural gift for Sequential Reasoning. The massive ICEE enterprise comprises many moving and unpredictable parts, including eight hundred repair technicians who report to ninety-nine different service centers nationwide. A former Green Beret, Leggett honed his organization and efficiency skills in the military, which he likens to his new civilian mission of overseeing ICEE's operations. "Managing multiple detachments in Syria is remarkably similar to running a call center for ICEE," he says.

Figuring out how to route and answer two thousand service requests with only twelve customer service representatives is fun for him. As a Sequential Thinker, Leggett takes a measured, logical, and deliberate approach to problems like this. Like Day, he loves "to solve wicked, complex problems," first by digesting huge amounts of information.[7] Recognizing the potential contributions of each person on his team, he deftly develops a plan and pinpoints which people should work together to reach a company goal.

Sequential Thinkers like Leggett are much-needed assets in entrepreneurial organizations where pivoting and navigating unexpected contingencies are the norm. They don't shrink from the opportunity to create a new system from scratch or without the help of a playbook. If you feel comfortable building the plane as you are flying it, you are likely gifted with this important aptitude. (With their talent for orchestrating complex systems with ease, we imagine legendary commanders and generals such as Winston Churchill and George Patton and film directors including Francis and Sofia Coppola all scoring as Sequential Thinkers.)

Sequential Thinker Challenges

Do you ever get dirty looks or pointed remarks about the state of your desk from your partner, roommate, or colleagues? If the papers on your desk are an unruly heap rather than a tidy stack, but you always know exactly where to find that sticky note with the sign-in password, it's because as a Sequential Thinker, everything is cataloged in your mental filing cabinet. Many who score at the right end of this aptitude continuum are slow to adopt organizational tools, simply because it's easier for them to mentally keep track of things. But there is a danger: when your brain shifts into overload and your effectiveness diminishes, you could discover that you need a bit of organizational help after all.

Communication can be a big challenge for people with this aptitude. The assumption that others are psychics or mind readers can trip you up and lead to frustration, particularly in partnerships or on teams. Zach Leggett recalls looking at the Green Beret recruits under his command in the military and thinking, *Why don't they get what I'm trying to say? Why aren't they doing this the way I asked?* He came to realize that if he failed to articulate his thoughts, no one would follow, so he made it a priority to improve.

"Showing your work" can feel laborious, but being able to clearly express your strategy to others is essential because any plan, however brilliant, can never be realized without supporters. While every step of a process is clear in Ben Day's mind, he's had trouble trying to explain to longshoremen why some spots have to be left open for the additional cargo to be loaded at the next port.

John Hamm, a former general partner at the venture capital firm VSP Capital, has noted how high-reliability teams such as emergency room staff or SWAT teams have "no room for sloppy communication. If team members don't speak to each other with precision, people die."[8] By taking pains to clearly define their expectations, terminology, the scope of work, and time line, Sequential Thinkers can make sure the glorious master plans floating in their heads will actually materialize into practical solutions.

If you're a Sequential Thinker, we recommend you devote careful attention to translating your internal strategic maps effectively for others. One common danger is to fall back on clichés such as "Customers come first," or "Full-court press." In managing his repair team, Leggett has found that such loose expressions lack critical detail and direction, forcing team members to make up their own minds about specific next steps.

At ICEE, Leggett has taken pains to slow down, find common ground, and carefully shepherd his team through the steps he so clearly envisions. One of his earlier methods was to write out his mental processes on whiteboards and sticky notes, then take photographs of them to share with others.

Since then, his wife has tried to help him transition to an electronic system known as Rocketbook, but the sticky-note habit has been tough to break. "I still have little notes stuck all over my office," Leggett laughs.

"On my birthday, my team wallpapered my door with hundreds of neon Post-its."

As the following story demonstrates, Betsy isn't a Sequential Thinker, but she is most certainly married to one. Most would agree that her architect husband, Ridley, is hyper-organized. But they don't know the half of it. At the end of each day, his email inbox is empty and his desk has the calm serenity of a desert plain. His work requires that he manage a zillion details and communicate them to the large network of tradespeople who will make his building plans a reality. As a Sequential Thinker, he constructs a mental map of each step needed to execute his designs, but he learned early on in his training that little can happen unless those sequences are memorialized into step-by-step plans on paper for others to see. Leveraging communication tools and systems has enabled his business to grow and he eagerly incorporates them into every aspect of their lives.

A dedicated scheduler, he sends Betsy a calendar invite for everything. *Everything.* Dental appointment? Calendar invite. Flight departure? Calendar invite. Flight change? New calendar invite. If she mentions she'll be stopping by Whole Foods on the way home from work to pick up some items for dinner, there is a good chance there will be a calendar invite. But on one memorable occasion, they experienced a system failure.

Betsy had spent six weeks planning a dinner party and had invited each guest by email: Wednesday, June 27, 7:00 p.m. But as it turned out June 27 was actually a Thursday. When she later realized her mistake, she assumed she had gotten the date wrong but the day of the week right. So, without consulting Ridley, she revised the event notification on their calendar to Wednesday, June 26.

As practiced hosts, they typically have time to relax with a glass of wine before their guests arrive. Wednesday evening around 7:45 p.m., Ridley asked, "How can everyone be so late?" "How strange," Betsy replied.

At last, it dawned on them—as they sat there with the table set, flowers arranged, and food simmering in the oven—that they'd begun the soiree *24 hours too early*. Turns out she had gotten the *day* of the week wrong, not the *date*, on the original invitation.

Within minutes, Ridley sent out a new calendar invite for the following night and gently chided Betsy to stay in her lane when it comes to scheduling. The following evening, everyone got a good laugh hearing about their "dress rehearsal" dinner party.

Sequential Thinkers at Work

The best careers for Sequential Thinkers feature a steady flow of information or problems that call for organization and strategy. If you have this aptitude, you thrive in environments that demand not just the implementation of solutions, but the use of logic and the crafting of new procedures. Seeking to maximize this aptitude, look for work that will allow you to plan and devise new and improved approaches to situations and challenges, such as software development, event planning, and any type of writing. (See the Appendix for some examples of job types and other activities that align with those who score as Sequential Thinkers.)

The Process Supporter

"A conductor without an orchestra," as the saying goes, "is just a person standing in a room waving a stick." Similarly, Sequential Thinkers are mere stick wavers without Process Supporters, crucial team members on whom they depend to help carry out their plans.

Process Supporters find their freedom within the boundaries of an established system; they appreciate order, strict protocol, and clear communication. If you score as a Process Supporter, you find taking meticulous steps and following orders immensely gratifying. You do your best work when there are set parameters. In many occupations (medical transcription, pharmacology, mechanical engineering, law, and so on) the precision of your work can mean the difference between life and death.

Consider Heather Holler, a thirty-four-year-old Hyundai Motorsports mechanic whose team relies upon her to, among other critical responsibilities, change race car tires at lightning speed. At the 2022 World Rally Championship in Croatia, the best drivers from around the world speed, skid, jump, and roll past villages of raucous onlookers and fields of indifferent dairy cows. "It's freaking crazy," she laughs. Typically, her crew is assigned to one car for the duration of the rally. "We each have a corner," she explains, "and then there are the specialists: the composite guy who does the carbon fiber pieces and a gearbox guy."

When one of their cars speeds—or sputters—into the service station, Holler and the other specialists put their process skills to work according to a well-rehearsed plan. For a sizzling quarter of an hour, Holler's tattooed forearms fly as she considers both minute mechanical details and the complex relationship among the car's various systems, including its engine, electronics, brakes, suspension, aerodynamics, and safety mechanisms. At that moment, sticking to the process is crucial; a mistake could mean driver injury or penalties. Like brain surgeons delicately undertaking a tumor removal, she and the other mechanics have to stay absolutely in the moment, hyper-focused on what they are doing. "If you're not really *there*," says Holler, pointing to her temple, "it's not good; people could die."[9]

Behind Every Rally Car Lies a Scrutineer

At the beginning and end of each rally, the race cars sit in the *parc fermé*, an off-limits locked lot where official teams of "scrutineers" meticulously check every car. They are looking for any hint of a broken safety protocol, cheating, or breach of regulation. Like so many worker bees, they verify required specs and parameters. They use a strict template to assess every aspect of the car, right down to the strictly regulated weight and millimeter dimensions of individual parts.

The scrutineers enforce accountability and ensure that all the finest details of the game plan slip into place, allowing both cars and their teams to run safely and smoothly. They are the Process Supporters. At the opposite extreme are the engineers, the Sequential Thinkers who rapidly grasp a problem, break it into its most pertinent parts, and mentally arrange those parts into a logical strategy that the mechanics, or Collaborative Planners, can then translate into reality. Serving as both sounding boards and practitioners, the mechanics work out how the plan will work in action.

Process Supporters are the people who really do let the cake cool before icing it because they know shortcuts can disappoint. While a company might rely on a Sequential Thinker to create a strategy to improve overall efficiency, the Process Supporter guarantees consistency. She knows when it's time to implement specific changes, scale up, or methodically carry out a new system across multiple corporate offices.

An indispensable member of any team, the Process Supporter can be relied upon to meticulously follow any hundred-step routine. The first person Zach Leggett hired when he started working at ICEE was Dan Thompson—a man who does not take shortcuts. When he receives a customer repair order from a Nebraska convenience store with a broken

ICEE machine, Thompson carefully tracks the status and communications for each stage of the process until the solution is implemented. He makes sure customers are kept up to date on each stage of their repair, and that not a single step is skipped.

As a person on what Leggett calls the "front lines" of ICEE operations, Thompson solves complicated problems that can include countless discrete and methodical tasks. "Dan is consistent, reliable, and an ideal fit for this job. He knows the specifics of this system better than I do," Leggett insists. "There are clear, linear steps to follow, and Dan can be counted on to not skip a beat. If a step is being missed or ignored, you can count on Dan to bring it to your attention."[10]

Process Supporter Challenges

If you are a Process Supporter, consistency, standards, structure, and explicit parameters are your watchwords, and your tools are outlines, checklists, and timetables. If you work for enterprises undergoing rapid change, in a department in disarray, or have a boss who is a poor communicator, you will get frustrated and even burn out. Change or deviation from an established system or protocol can knock you off your game, so you need training and support when encountering new organizational systems or technologies. Likewise, if outmoded tools or burdensome processes aren't working for you, don't hesitate to advocate for upgrades, as these deliver great value to a team.

It is important to recognize the importance of structure in the lives of Process Supporters, both at work and at home. Remember that it's okay to ask your spouse, friends, supervisor, or co-workers to be specific with their directions when they are asking you for something, so that you can make sure you have all the necessary resources at hand. If, for example, your partner scheduled a busy Saturday packed with errands and playdates, nailing down exactly what your role will be at each stage of the day can help you plan. It's also a good idea to ask "how?" and "why?" even when it feels superfluous, because having granular knowledge of a process will help you to do your best.

Process Supporters at Work

Process Supporters make stellar and reliable partners. They are also the lifeblood of any organization. They can provide steady leadership in roles where rules are paramount and all growth is firmly rooted in established standards. Notable positions such as chief financial officer, chief counsel, and head of human resources are just a few jobs that Process Supporters might find rewarding. Whether you are a risk officer monitoring SEC compliance for a financial firm or a restaurant manager tasked with enforcing health inspector guidelines, this aptitude is key. (See the Appendix for some examples of job types and other activities that align with those who score as Process Supporters.)

The Collaborative Planner

Collaborative Planners are the indispensable managers of an enterprise. They are the people on whom Sequential Thinkers depend to flesh out the specifics of their plans and who uncover areas for improvement. It's common for Sequential Thinkers to enlist Collaborative Planners as sounding boards; the two often work in tandem to hash out a strategy or develop a step-by-step process. As codifiers, communicators, and clarifiers, Collaborative Planners make life easier for both Sequential Thinkers and Process Supporters. Their practical contributions bring a plan to life and up to scale. Their sweet spot is transforming the "pretty good" into something outstanding.

Before she retired, collaborative planner Mary Kenny *literally* got projects off the ground. A former account executive for Airship International, she spent a decade managing the operations of a massive helium blimp. Doing so involved coordinating a host of detailed logistics as the floating vessel and its support team of pilots, mechanics, electronics technicians, and ground service personnel traveled from state to state making appearances.

The "lighter than air" industry, as the blimp business is known to insiders, is relatively small, with fewer than twenty-five airships in circulation worldwide. Most people have seen a Goodyear blimp hovering over a stadium or a state fair, but few may know that these vessels were initially developed to support military objectives. Today, blimps are typically leased by the month by a company that wants to promote its brand and cost upward of $500,000 to operate. "The crew chief and the pilots set the course," Kenny recalls, "and I made sure their plan was supported. I didn't have to start from scratch."

While Sequential Thinkers like Zach Leggett lean toward thinking in broad strokes, nimbly creating a strategy, it is the bailiwick of the Collaborative Planner to fill in the plan with crucial information that can be used to coalesce the rest of the team. Kenny describes a typical engagement with a client as "an exercise in logistical gymnastics." Because blimps are always at the mercy of the weather, changes in plans are constant. For each trip, she kept the schedule with all of the hotel and other logistics information in three-ring binders, with page dividers for fallback options in cities along the route in case the crew couldn't make it to their destinations.

Once, the nation of Trinidad engaged a blimp to surveil drug trades. When she gave a binder with contingencies to the crew chief for the trip, he "looked at me like I was neurotic," she said. But the weather proved unkind, and the crew was forced to stop in the Dominican Republic on their way to deliver the ship. Because Kenny had planned for all possible scenarios, she quickly found accommodations for everyone soon after they anchored at the airport.[11]

Collaborative Planners are also natural teachers with a gift for bringing enthusiasm and a fresh take to familiar topics or lessons. Marcus Wright, a thirty-four-year-old owner of Northwest Dog Training in Seattle, Washington, made the decision to leap from financial services to canine training during the Covid-19 pandemic. Wright excels when working within the loose structure of a template, especially when there is the flexibility to tweak and improve it. His courses utilize approaches that he learned from older, accomplished trainers like his personal mentor, Bob Smith, an eighty-year-old with whom he spent hundreds of weekend hours. "The main thing I learned from hanging around trainers," he says, "is that there is not one way to train a dog. I take bits and pieces of different regimens and put them together. For some, I do positive reinforcement; others may require leash pressure concepts. I honestly don't care how the training gets done, as long as it's right for the dog."[12]

True to the nature of the Collaborative Planner, Wright doesn't need to reinvent the wheel. Established systems and playbooks are the scaffolding upon which Wright's creative expression and talent flourish.

Collaborative Planner Challenges

If you're a Collaborative Planner, you need a vibrant and evolving work environment in order to thrive. Like a Sequential Thinker, you enjoy creating and refining systems, but you can become frustrated when you feel as if your suggestions for improvement are not being heard or considered. And like a Process Supporter, you count on having some preexisting tools and structures in place to help you organize your thoughts and ideas. You will need to grab a pad of paper when you are engaged in a heavy exercise of mental planning, and a calendar when you need to prioritize your list of tasks.

Collaborative Planners at Work

Collaborative Planners are skilled at both coordinating a plan and following an existing one. They are also uniquely equipped to point out inefficiencies in how things are run at home or at work, and they enjoy taking a good project or strategy for approaching a problem and making it great. Their versatility helps them excel in roles that require both giving and taking direction such as consulting, training, teaching, and counseling. (See the Appendix for some examples of job types and other activities that align with those who score as Collaborative Planners.)

Who's Packing Your Parachute?

It takes a lot of people to create a great team. Whether we are Sequential Thinkers, Process Supporters, or Collaborative Planners, the most worthwhile projects and enterprises engage all three aptitude types. It is therefore incumbent upon leaders everywhere to acknowledge and appreciate the contribution of the many, from top-ranked managers to the people who cut the paychecks or handle the mail room.

Charlie Plumb has plenty to say on this topic. He had completed seventy-five combat missions as a US fighter pilot in Vietnam when he was shot down. Ejected from his F-4 Phantom jet, Plumb parachuted into enemy hands. He was captured, tortured, and imprisoned for 2,103 days before he was released.[13]

Years later, as he was dining with his wife in a restaurant, a man came up to him and said, "You're Plumb! You flew jet fighters in Vietnam from the aircraft carrier *Kitty Hawk*. You were shot down!" Confused, Plumb asked how the man knew so much about him. "I packed your parachute," the man replied, shaking Plumb's hand. "I guess it worked!"

Plumb assured him that it had. "If your chute hadn't worked, I wouldn't be here today."[14]

That night, Plumb couldn't sleep. He was thinking about the man who, during the Vietnam War, spent his hours carefully folding silk parachutes in the dark bowels of a navy ship, knowing that lives depended on their opening safely. "I wonder how many times I might have seen him and not even said 'Good morning, how are you?' or anything," Plumb recalled. "Because you see, I was a fighter pilot and he was just a sailor."

Charles Plumb is now a motivational speaker who has shared his story with thousands of audiences. And each time he tells it, he always asks: "Who's packing your parachute?"

Part III

The Amplifiers

Amplifiers are narrower, more specialized aptitudes that can behave like a pinch of salt, enhancing all the best flavors in your Core Four. When combined with other natural abilities, Amplifiers can supercharge your performance and they can be critical to our success in a particular field.

Amplifiers are essential to some occupations and bonuses in others. The ability to withstand glaring light is an invaluable asset for truck drivers. A microsurgeon should be adept at finger dexterity, and the women who play in the WNBA need exceptional hand-eye coordination. A lucky few have a rare amplifier that signals profound talent: think of Mariah Carey and her five-octave, perfect-pitch vocal range.

CHAPTER 7

Visual Comparison Speed and Numerical Reasoning

It is for us to pray not for tasks equal to our powers, but for powers equal to our tasks.

—Helen Keller

Visual Comparison Speed and Numerical Reasoning are two Amplifiers that have a profound impact on our performance of essential tasks. A score on the right end of these continuums can be considered a plus. In general, it indicates a preference for using the aptitude more frequently, a fact that goes unnoticed by many who engage it automatically. If your score lands closer to the middle or left side of these continuums, don't be dismayed, because this realization will also unlock valuable insights and improve your efficacy in activities throughout your life.

Visual Comparison Speed

VISUAL COMPARISON SPEED

Double Checker	‹ ‹ ‹ ‹ ‹	List Checker	› › › › ›	Visual Scanner

Whether we're perusing texts and emails or looking over tax forms, PowerPoint presentations, apartment rental agreements, healthcare questionnaires, performance evaluations, or invoices, it's impossible to avoid paperwork (or more commonly today, computer work). Scoring on the right end of the Visual Comparison Speed continuum indicates that you find performing these kinds of administrative tasks easy and fast, while a score on the left means you find them tedious and time-consuming.

The Exercise

In this exercise you'll be presented with two long columns of numbers and asked to compare them. Within a short time frame, you will fill in a box between the numbers with an *L* for like and a *D* for different.

56	D	65
9243561	L	9243561
87354	L	87354
57165239	☐	57162539
1432		1432

Visual Scanners breeze through the exercise, completing all of the items with precision. List Checkers also complete the activity, but make frequent errors along the way. Double Checkers struggle to finish the exercise within the time limit albeit with a high degree of accuracy.

A natural talent for spotting anomalies can save lives if you are an EMT, an anesthesiologist, a pharmacist, a nuclear equipment technician, a police officer, or an air traffic controller. It also comes in handy if you happen to work with DNA.

Dr. Stephenie Riley, a natural medicine doctor in the small mountain town of Truckee, California, scans results from a genetic testing kit as another source of data to supplement annual blood panels and patient office visits. Riley regularly exercises her Visual Scanning aptitude by combing through the sixty-six-page 23andMe report, with its seemingly unending rows of alleles (AA, GG, TT, CC) swirling in her brain. (An allele is one of two or more versions of a gene or a segment of a DNA sequence that occurs at a specific location in the genome. An individual inherits two alleles, one from each parent. Determining whether, and where, these two alleles match reveals the genetic profile of a given individual.) With her hawklike eyes, Riley finds enormous satisfaction in hunting down anomalies like a kestrel hunts mice in the grass. She highlights each marker that might signal a red flag, or simply something of interest, and then shares her insights with the patient. "I'm sort of conditioned to spot constellations of markers," she admitted. But that's not all. As a Diagnostic Problem Solver, she also enjoys asking why. "I like to figure out what's driving those markers. What's the story behind them?"[1]

One Disastrous Typo

In some cases, failing to spot tiny anomalies can lead to catastrophic consequences. For example, consider what happened when the phone rang in Philip Davison-Sebry's peaceful hotel room one February morning in 2009.

Davison-Sebry and his wife, Cherrie, had been enjoying an idyllic and long-anticipated trip to the Maldives to celebrate Cherrie's fiftieth birthday, unaware that 4,500 miles away at their home in Wales, the business in which he served as managing director was in free fall. The company Davison-Sebry led, Taylor & Sons Ltd., had been founded by his family 124 years prior, employed over 250 people, and served customers spanning the globe. The company's financial picture was solid and its pipeline of orders was robust, with projected revenue of over £40 million (over $50 million). The last person Davison-Sebry expected to hear on the other end of the line while on his holiday was an irate customer, whose anger shot through the receiver like a spear.

"What are you doing away at a time like this?" the man demanded. "Your company is in liquidation!"

At first, the managing director thought the call was a practical joke, perhaps set up by a colleague. But within a few hours, it was evident that something had gone wrong, *very* wrong. It took less than three days to identify the cause of the meltdown but, sadly, it was too late to reverse the colossal damage from an avalanche of canceled orders and withdrawn credit.

What precipitated the collapse?

It turns out that an employee at Companies House, the executive agency sponsored by the Department for Business, Energy and Industrial Strategy, had unintentionally ignited the explosion with a single keystroke. Companies House is responsible for recording new and dissolving limited companies and making that information available to the public. An extra "s" had been mistakenly keyed at the end of the name of a *different* company, Taylor & Son Ltd., which was in fact dissolving. The error was made worse because the agency routinely sold the information to credit reference agencies. Once the employee pressed send, the incorrect information was spread instantly over the internet, making the damage all but impossible to rectify. In essence, the company's reputation was forever sullied because of a single typo. The tiny error resulted in a lawsuit and ultimately a judgment in favor of Taylor & Sons Ltd. for £8.8 million (over $11 million). Still, more than 250 people were left without employment, and productive years were lost in court in order to reach a settlement.[2]

The ubiquity and occasionally catastrophic consequences of clerical errors make proofreading an essential undertaking. Good proofreaders would have prevented the Taylor & Sons catastrophe and other notable blunders, such as the minting of six thousand papal medals by the Vatican that had to be pulled from circulation due to "Jesus" being misspelled as "Lesus."[3]

On rare occasions, a mistake produces unexpected gains. The first edition of *Harry Potter and the Philosopher's Stone* went off to press with a typo on its back cover ("Philospher's Stone," instead of "Philosopher's Stone"), making it an instant collector's item (copies of that edition are now worth hundreds of thousands of dollars).[4] And when two graduate students at Stanford, Larry Page and Sergey Brin, first began brainstorming names for their new search engine, another classmate, Sean Anderson, suggested "googolplex," referring to a 1 followed by googol zeros, and they landed on simply "googol," or a 1 followed by 100 zeros. When Anderson did a quick search to make sure the domain name "googol.com" did not already exist, he typed in "google.com" by mistake. Page loved it, and so the name "Google" came into being.[5] But ultimately, typos cost more than they're worth, so it's best to catch them early and often.

The Proof Is in the Proofing

It's easy to assume that our tendency to make typos stems from a lack of focus. *What a silly mistake*, you might say, or *How careless*. In fact, the ubiquity of typos has to do with the inner workings of the brain. As psychologist Tom Stafford has noted, "When you're writing, you're trying to convey meaning. It's a very high-level task."[6] The ability to generalize about the meaning of our writing, therefore, takes the larger share of our brain power and dominates our thinking, even to the extent that we can proofread our own work and not catch errors that might be glaringly obvious to someone else. Preoccupied with what we are saying, our brains can frequently miss the finer details of how what we're thinking is physically written. Yet this natural propensity for generalizing also plays a critical role in helping us navigate a complex and fast-paced world. For example: *Yuo cna porbalby raed tihs esaliy despite teh msispeillgns.* This ability to grasp the broader point is what allows us to effectively skim through news articles, road signs, or work emails.

The List Checkers and Double Checkers who sit elsewhere on this continuum can master efficient copyediting, but compared to Visual Scanners they will require additional time and effort, and many may prefer to focus their efforts elsewhere. While List Checkers catch the most errors when they are working at a steady pace, Double Checkers benefit from eye breaks and also might need more time to reread and verify.

Regardless of whether you score as a Visual Scanner, List Checker, or Double Checker, your awareness of this aptitude will give you a clear picture of how much time you will need to both avoid and correct clerical mistakes. It's also important to remember that when looking for potentially costly errors is called for, accuracy trumps speed. Judy Beaver, the founder of National Proofreading Day (which takes place every year on March 8), happens to be a proud middle-to-left-end Visual Comparison Speed scorer and she has thrived in her role as a proofreader and a proofreading advocate. For someone who has dedicated her life to promoting proofreading, she takes a surprisingly plodding approach when reviewing a document. "I'm a slow reader," she explains. "I tend to read every word like I'm reading out loud in my head, so I see typos and punctuation mistakes."[7] As the National Proofreading Day website notes, "mistakes make us look bad," and it "feels great" to fix an error. It's also "an easy way to help a friend." Whether, like Judy, we find proofreading to be a pleasure or an arduous chore, in the modern era we have myriad tools such as autocorrect, spell-check, Grammarly, voice recognition, and others to help refine our written expression.

When You're Forced to Be Fast

If you score on the left-hand end of the Visual Comparison Speed continuum, you could be unaware of how everyday administrative tasks pile up if not attended to right away. In allowing invoices, expense account receipts, and bills to stack up, you can bring about late fees (and attendant anxiety). When you are forced to rush by addressing these things at the last minute, you may find that your work is riddled with mistakes. One strategy is to offload some of these tasks to others who are in the middle of the continuum or on the right-hand side, and instead volunteer for more suitable assignments, giving your other aptitudes an opportunity to flourish.

Where you land on this aptitude continuum may also provide insight into past performance on academic tests. Unfortunately, conventional schooling relies in part on timed, written examinations that employ multiple-choice or short-answer questions to measure achievement. Similarly, time is almost always a factor in high-stakes standardized tests, so visual scanning speed can penalize some test takers while helping others. Scores on these tests might not reflect the learning accomplishments of the eager student who relishes in-class discussions or take-home assignments. The good news is that most occupations in the real world will allow you to approach your clerical tasks at your natural pace.

Even so, the early years of many careers come laden with clerical assignments. If a manager is herself a Visual Scanner, she should view her score as an exception and be cautioned to look beneath the hood before labeling her subordinates as "lazy" or "careless." Understanding this aptitude and its relative value can prevent the loss of real talent caused by a job function mismatch. The data analyst who is rapidly graying and hurtling toward burnout while laboring over detailed spreadsheets day after day may, in fact, turn out to be a rock star in business development. All she needs is an opportunity.

Numerical Reasoning

NUMERICAL REASONING

Numerical Checker	‹ ‹ ‹ ‹	Numerical Predictor	› › › ›	Numerical Detective

Numerical Reasoning is an aptitude for applied mathematics—that is, the degree of comfort that you feel when identifying connections, trends, or patterns in numbers. For some, the language of numbers is a mother tongue and a "go-to" channel for solving problems, especially those of a practical nature. Statistics, predictive analytics, forecasting, and budgeting are just a few uses for this aptitude.

The Exercise

In this exercise you'll be asked to choose the number that should come next in a series. The exercise begins with easier sequences, such as the one below, or: *2, 4, 6, 8, 10, __?* a pattern of +2. Then it advances to more challenging patterns such as: *1, 3, 9, 27, 81, __?* in a pattern of ×3, like this:

20	19	17	14	10	__
A	15				
B	7				
C	9				
D	6				
E	5				

Numerical Detectives find this kind of trend-hunting both fun and fascinating. They love thinking about numerical patterns and the concepts behind them. They can solve problems like the one above in their heads, and mathematical explanations or solutions come easily to them, regardless of the size of the problem. They use numbers as a tool when sorting through information in their personal and professional lives.

A Numerical Predictor can, given enough time, figure out what the next number would be. Not all, but many who score on the far left of the continuum, Numerical Checkers, find the exercise so arduous that, midway through, they may just randomly guess at the answers.

Much like the core aptitude of Spatial Visualization, Numerical Reasoning can go unrecognized in compulsory schooling. So, unless you were lucky enough to take statistics or economics in high school, you probably wouldn't know whether you have this gift. If you scored as a Numerical Detective and don't currently use math daily, consider developing this aptitude further. You could have an inner data scientist just waiting to be freed.

Today's data scientists are like magicians, and powerful computers are their magic wands. Immersed in vast online depositories of information, they get a kick out of readily discerning phenomena that others can't immediately see. Their work has improved practically all aspects of the human experience, from finding matches between available kidneys to those needing lifesaving transplants, to preventing the wrongful incarceration of the mentally ill. Some data science teams have discovered that 5:00 p.m. is prime time for substance abuse and that Monday is the most challenging day for eating disorders. Thanks to their analyses, we now know that texts containing the word *ibuprofen* are sixteen times more likely to require an active rescue situation for local responders.[8] By crafting complex, upscaled solutions based on mathematical algorithms, data scientists can predict what's going to happen in the future.

D. J. Patil has a gift for Numerical Reasoning. By his own description, this data scientist is "terrible at arithmetic." Nevertheless, he is exceptionally skilled at seeing, identifying, and using complex numerical patterns. "I'm not interested in the *calculations* of numbers," Patil explained to us. "But I can tell you all sorts of interesting things about the *relationships* among sets of numbers."[9] Engaging in rote mental math utterly bores him, but he relishes the opportunity to tackle a real-world problem by pattern-matching swarms of choreographed numbers, which is what data science is all about.

So, if you've always assumed that you are terrible at math but score as a Numerical Detective, think again. It's possible you have untapped potential opportunities to explore.

One of Alex's favorite moments of her job is when she gets to share Numerical Reasoning results with clients. Wary of unpleasant experiences with mathematics in high school or college, they have often spent years convincing themselves they are not "math people." But, for the first time, their test results prove them wrong.

For example, Simon,[10] a high school student in Chicago, can hardly recall a time when he didn't need extra help in math. He spends hours with a tutor each Monday after school. As a junior, he is now doubling down in preparation for the high-stakes college entrance exams, and the quantitative sections are just one more gauntlet to clear. He was understandably surprised to discover his strong Numerical Reasoning aptitude, but Alex explained that the math concepts he'd been learning in school were not putting this particular gift to good use. He has yet to embrace his applied mathematical powers and let them shine. But "Just wait until you take statistics next year," she told him. "That's where you'll really see this aptitude at work."

The Destructive Force of Math Anxiety

It's helpful to distinguish an aptitude for applied math from its close cousin, Numerical Computation. The latter is taught in compulsory math courses. While some struggle to grasp algebra and calculus concepts and suffer from math anxiety, they find applied math, such as the kind Patil deploys, a pleasure.

Unfortunately for a large percentage of the population, the very mention of math wields a particular triggering power. Starting as early as elementary school, math anxiety can linger throughout life and become a generational inheritance, as parents pass their negative feelings on to their children. A staggering 93 percent of American adults have reported feeling apprehensive about mathematical concepts.[11] To make matters worse, biases that feed negative self-perception can erode our confidence as well as our performance in math.

Alex has a distinct memory of participating in a psychology study as a college freshman. It was a mandatory assignment for Psych 101 students and, like many psychology experiments, it shared precious little information with its study subjects. A required consent informed them that the experiment would not cause any physical or psychological harm. But they didn't know exactly what was being studied or how they would be evaluated.

The experiment began with a graduate student handing Alex a packet of photocopied news articles. She told Alex to read each article and complete the assignment on the packet's final page. Easy enough, she thought. So, she sat down to read.

Before long, a common theme emerged. In some way or another, each of the articles cast a negative light on women. With every turn of the page, she became more and more uncomfortable, and even a little angry, and she dreaded reading the next one. She started clenching her jaw and chewing her lip, as she often does in stressful situations.

Relieved to finish the final article, she turned to the last page only to discover, to her horror, that the assignment was a math problem. With sweaty palms and a dry mouth, she scanned the words. "Come on, you can do this," she told herself. But she had suddenly forgotten how to do even the simplest arithmetic.

Furious, exhausted, and embarrassed, she scribbled down some awful, cobbled-together guesses and handed them to the graduate student. Only then did she learn the purpose of the experiment. The researchers were trying to understand how negative labels, biases, and derogatory remarks affect a woman's academic performance. Does being degraded, repeatedly and over time, impact our confidence in ourselves and our work? For Alex, at least, the answer was a resounding yes.

A person's subjective beliefs and feelings can be heavily influenced by societal messages that come at the price of missed opportunities, underemployment, and lost wage potential. Nowhere is this more apparent than in STEM fields. In the 2017 to 2018 school year, women represented only 22 percent of degree recipients in engineering and 19 percent in computer science. But the opportunities are not just out of view for women; people of color also remain underrepresented in the STEM workforce. According to a Pew Research Center analysis of a community survey taken between 2017 and 2019, only 5 percent of Black workers and 9 percent of Latinx workers occupied engineering jobs.[12]

We need to fix this math gap, and fast. Dismissing math-based careers such as data science due to a misunderstanding of your numerical potential is a mistake, so we encourage you to go back to the starting line, where you left your numerical confidence, and reconsider.

Using Math in the Real World

When they learn their score, Numerical Detectives often reflect on times when they've used their aptitude casually, without thinking anything of it. Perhaps you're the type who is glued to the screen tracking returns on election night; or you look forward to fantasy football season to exercise your natural grasp of player statistics. You're the one who started the college investment club and still relish keeping abreast of economic news. The Bloomberg phone app has a permanent spot on your home screen.

If you score at or near the middle of the Numerical Reasoning continuum, you're likely to take longer to understand the logic behind numerical sequences, especially if it's the first time you've seen a particular pattern. Don't let this deter you from exploring jobs that involve some degree of number wrangling. Once you become familiar with a process or algorithm, the rest will flow.

According to the jobs site Glassdoor, some of the top skills needed for today's tech jobs include time series analysis, statistical modeling, and machine learning.[13] All of these tasks require some level of confidence with numbers. Even beyond the world of tech, jobs and positions that specialize in working with big data are on the rise. So don't dismiss your suitability for occupations based on your prior assumptions or past experiences that have eroded your math confidence.

Regardless of whether you are a Numerical Detective, Predictor, or Checker, it's crucial to incorporate the principles of applied math into your life. Much like riding a bike, being able to read a balance sheet, grasp statistical patterns, or interpret data related to your interests is an essential skill everyone should cultivate. You don't have to be a data jockey like D. J. Patil, but taking time to familiarize yourself with the basics of accounting and becoming competent with tools like Quick-Books or Excel will increase your savvy and elevate your position in every arena. Learning the essentials may be as simple as getting some coaching from a friend or trusted mentor.

Once you build the bridge between abstract numbers and real-life problems, you can walk into your workplace, and into the world, feeling empowered. You might, for example, figure out how the numbers tell a story about your spending habits, your potential future business earnings, or your child's college savings fund. In tackling all of these challenges and many more, Numerical Reasoning is your ally, and not your enemy.

The Legacy of Latin Squares

Flipping (or scrolling) through the games section of your favorite news source, do you ever gravitate toward the Sudoku section? With an apti-tude for Numerical Reasoning, you can not only memorize but also re-call and apply numerical facts from diverse sources with ease. You excel at using data to make accurate estimates and projections, and you thrive in roles that depend on instantaneous, real-time access to important numerical information. Sudoku and other number-based games and puzzles feel like an energizing jog in the park to those on the right end of the Numerical Reasoning continuum.

In 1783, a Swiss mathematician named Leonhard Euler created what he called a "new kind of magic squares" known as "Latin Squares." The rules of the game involved filling a grid of squares with symbols or num-bers but only allowing each figure to appear once in each row or column.

This early template floated around for two hundred years before catching the eye of a small New York publishing company, Dell Magazines. Calling it Number Place, Dell began publishing the puzzles and by the 1980s a publisher in Japan saw its potential. They made two small improvements and gave it a new name, Sudoku (in Japanese, *su* means "number" and *doku* means "singular" or "unique"). The puzzle now consisted of a nine-by-nine-inch square grid. Each row and column had to be filled with the numbers one through nine, with no repeats.

Sudoku first began its ascent to fame when New Zealand expatriate Wayne Gould picked one up in a Tokyo bookstore. An instant fan, Gould spent six years creating a new computer program for generating original Sudoku, and decided to try publishing them in a local newspaper in Conway, New Hampshire, where his wife lived. Soon the British paper *The Times* picked them up, too, and the puzzles caught fire worldwide.[14] Numerical Detectives find it especially satisfying to use their logic and ability to spot numerical patterns to solve Sudoku, but Numerical Predictors and even some Numerical Checkers can also enjoy the challenge of tackling these puzzles.

In the end, flexing our Numerical Reasoning muscles through games like Sudoku can be beneficial and fun even if doing so isn't necessary; psychiatrists have found that it helps keep our brains in shape as we age.[15] These Amplifiers can also help break the tie when your driving aptitudes are pointing you equally in two different directions. While Visual Comparison Speed and Numerical Reasoning are two of the most prominent Amplifiers, a host of others can bring additional insights to help you recognize and maximize your personal strengths.

CHAPTER 8

Cherries on Top:
The Other Amplifiers

"Learn like a bird, create tools, and improve your abilities."
—Dil Nawaz

There are a host of specialized abilities that provide an extra boost when combined with your Core Four, but to assess all of them would take an exorbitant amount of time. We'll focus on a few of the more common of these amplifiers, starting with the ones included in your assessment. Like the cherries that top off a sundae, they aren't absolutely critical, but they can garnish your potential and can give you an edge in performing certain tasks. But whether these come easily to you or not, modern technology has given us myriad digital tools which will come to your rescue.

Perhaps the biggest technology-enabled advances relate to memory. No longer are you expected to mentally store the password to your on-line banking application, the day of your child's musical, or the name of your dog's veterinarian. Once absolutely crucial to climbing the academic ladder of success, some memory aptitudes are now of marginal utility. Still, they can come in handy when you don't happen to have a digital device at the ready.

Mysterious Memory

In the ancient story of *The Odyssey*, the long-suffering hero, Odysseus, strives to return home after ten years of war in Troy. On his journey, he spends another ten years fighting sea monsters, angry gods, a man-eating cyclops, a seductive witch, and more. When at last Odysseus washes ashore on his beloved island home of Ithaca, he finally falls into the arms of his equally long-suffering wife, Penelope.

Universally recognized as one of the great literary works of ancient Greece and first documented in the seventh century BCE, this epic poem fills twenty-four books and 12,109 lines of dactylic hexameter.[1] Since the poem was originally *sung*, not written, it might take some twenty hours to perform. In a miraculous feat, ancient bards must have strung together dozens of verses and phrases in musical form so they could sing this immense and marvelous recitation entirely from memory.[2]

Although *The Odyssey* is attributed to a single person we call Homer today, many scholars believe the poem was distilled from the oral traditions of ancient singer-poets (or *aoidoi*) before the Greeks developed a written language.[3] Like the choruses of a song, certain elements in *The Odyssey* repeat ("bright-eyed Athena," "wine-dark sea," "rosy-fingered dawn," and so on), helping the singer to remember the story.[4] If you have a terrific memory and want to entertain and amaze your friends for hours on end, these cues and other patterns in the rhythm and words would help you absorb and memorize the entire poem.

Today, the extraordinary art of reciting at length from memory has shrunk down to a specialized form of performance. Otherwise, anyone interested in speaking or singing Homer's lines can read them from a screen. But as one of humanity's greatest and most mysterious attributes, memorization remains a boon for singers and actors, and it's a superb tool for acquiring foreign languages or cramming for tests.

By contrast, have you ever been puzzled—or annoyed—by what your friends and loved ones do or don't remember? Some people appear to be selective memorizers, choosing to absorb and recall only that which is important to them. *Why does my partner remember everyone's name after each party we attend, but never our anniversary? How can my son remember every baseball statistic, yet constantly forget about his homework?*

The assessment tests three distinct types of memory that affect the ways you learn, work, and interact with others. By gaining a better understanding of how your memory functions, you can recognize and harness your own memorization style.

For example, consider the first concert you ever attended with friends. You were all together at the same place and at the same time— yet if asked about it later, each of you will remember different aspects of the experience. You might recall each of the names and facts about not just the feature band, but the obscure new group that opened the show. Perhaps your friend who booked the tickets recalls exactly how much a seat had cost, or what the order confirmation number was. Maybe your little sister, who tagged along that night, drew a picture in her sketchbook of the concert stadium when she got back home; and she can still, even now, create an image of the stadium that looks almost like the real thing. You showed your knack for Associative Memory by recalling details about the opening band after skimming through a single article on them. Your friend demonstrated Visual Memory by effortlessly remembering the ticket price and the confirmation number. Your sister displayed Pattern Memory with her perfect sketch of the concert stadium.

Associative Memory was Homer's strength.[5] View your score on this assessment as an indicator of how much exposure you need to new terminology or a foreign vocabulary word before you can accurately retain and recall it. Some can lock down a term or fact with a single impression. Others require conscious practice and repetition to remember it.

Unfortunately for many, this little Amplifier makes a big difference in conventional schooling that relies heavily on repeated recitation and memorization, especially in the primary years. After all, ABCs and multiplication tables are building blocks for reading and math. If associative memory is one of your strengths, you might remember being the first to raise your hand when the teacher asked a question, or secretly enjoying pop quizzes. If memorizing your lines for the school play was a breeze, consider yourself fortunate.

Historically a signal of superior "wit" and intelligence, the ability to recall information quickly reaps high marks and praise from parents and teachers. Yet an unfortunate consequence of this recognition is the under-valuing of other types of memory processing. Indeed, if it normally takes you more repetition and effort than others to secure a word or fact in your long-term memory vault, you may have spent your childhood mistakenly convinced that you were less intelligent than your peers. The resulting damage to your self-esteem can be lasting, even though other aptitudes such as Inductive Reasoning, Sequential Reasoning, and Idea Generation gain more purchase than Associative Memory by sixth or seventh grade. Without adequate recognition of their intelligence or encouragement from adults, many children give up or lose interest in school because their brains aren't built for instant recall. For others who mustered the stamina and drive to persevere, it takes extra commitment to find memorization strategies to carry them through years of traditional schooling.

Today, the field of education is finally moving toward a more personalized approach to learning, and teachers have eagerly embraced an array of methods that meet the individual needs of learners. Songs, mnemonic devices (the funnier, the better), poems, stories, and word-picture association memory aids are just a few approaches that alleviate the grind of rote memorization.

Social media is also playing an important role, engaging people of all ages in continuous learning on topics ranging from historical facts to language acquisition.

The importance of building a robust vocabulary cannot be overstated, and the means of acquiring it differs from person to person. While not an aptitude, vocabulary is included in the YouScience assessment. A learned skill, word knowledge enhances our ability to communicate effectively and contributes to work confidence. Whatever your current level, Solid, Accomplished, or Masterful, new words are always a joy to acquire. And if you know where to look, the process can be downright entertaining.

We caught up with one social media phenom, Beverly Mahone, known to her global audience as "Auntie Bev," whose engaging TikToks and Instagram posts have swept millions of followers into her vocabulary fun house. A vocabulary cognoscenti (discerning expert) behind the company All Wordz Matter, she knows those vocab flashcards you practiced in school were a drag. Keenly aware that people go on TikTok to be amused, "and they don't really want to sit and listen to Auntie Bev give them a five-minute lesson on vocabulary," she cleverly employs myriad tricks to help people retain information, knowing that it's the "stickiness" of a concept that determines whether we'll remember it or not. In one post she coyly begins with an unexpected question, "Have you ever heard anyone refer to someone else as a pussy?" She goes on to explain that the reason may be because they couldn't pronounce the actual word, *pusillanimous* ("coward"). Others of these bite-size social media videos feature her in unexpected settings to dramatize the lesson. For example, the scene of a car accident prompted an opportunity to present the word *impede* ("to delay or prevent by obstruction"). She understands that for visual learners, the ability to link a mental image with the vocabulary is especially helpful.

Auntie Bev's clever approaches have yielded a million-plus social media followers, mostly thirty-somethings who tune in to her word-of-the-day. She advises, "If people want to grow their vocabulary, first try to guess the meaning of a word in a text by reading the sentence before and following the unfamiliar word to see if you can derive the meaning from context. Then, look up the word to see how close you are." Over time, this discipline will plant new words into your long-term memory because you'll associate the word with what you read or saw or experienced. Now sixty-six, Auntie Bev has practiced this technique her whole life, accumulating some twenty journals with words and definitions that have become familiar acquaintances in her daily speech.

For Auntie Bev, a big vocabulary is more than a parlor trick; the effort you put into memorizing a varied word bank will pay dividends throughout your life, giving you a seat at the table and the satisfaction of understanding and feeling understood by others. "That's why I've tried to stress the importance of being able to articulate your thoughts," says Bev. "It gives you confidence. There have been times when I have been the only woman in the room—the only black person in the room—and I always felt I could hold my own because I knew how to communicate." It's no wonder that one of Auntie Bev's favorite words is "indomitable," meaning "impossible to defeat." "I basically look in the mirror every morning and say, 'I am indomitable.'"

What we remember influences more than how we learn. It also impacts how we work and interact with others. You might, for example, be one of those people who just can't remember names. Or maybe you've become so reliant on using technology to remind you of things that your smartphone has become an extension of your body. If you need some help remembering something, don't be afraid to ask a friend or colleague, or to lean into digital tools. Finding places on your computer or other devices to store names, birthdates, important meetings, the quickest route to the hospital, and other bits of information will give you the freedom to focus on what matters most.

Visual Memory influences how easily you learn and accurately recall numerical data. People strong in this Amplifier can retrieve their childhood friend's birthday, their driver's license number, or their bank routing number in seconds. Tessa, a financial analyst with the University of California, told us that numbers "stuck" with her at an early age. As a child, she quickly memorized not only her own social security number but those of each of her family members.[6] People who can retain data this way keep numbers stored in their phone but prefer to manually punch in the digits instead, because it seems easier than finding the person's name in their contact list. In fact, they are likely to remember a phone number even better than a name. While they could use a digital "password keeper," they prefer to use the password filing system in their heads. Meanwhile, those who find it more challenging to retain this kind of information can count on digital address books, notes, and online applications to store all the visual memory they need.

Pattern Memory, a powerful complement to the Spatial Visualization aptitude, affects how well you absorb and recall visual surroundings. Those gifted with this Amplifier rapidly take in all the rich patterns in the physical environment, their eyes gravitating toward visual themes that others might miss. Their brains effortlessly catalog everything they see for later retrieval. These human cameras can link a certain dress cut to its decade of origin, or remember what style of jeans was "in" in 2006. They easily distinguish the Louis Vuitton fake from the real thing, and they're the first to notice when friends change their profile picture on their social media account.

Nate Smitherman, a junior at the American College of the Building Arts in Charleston, South Carolina, can recall his childhood home with stunning accuracy. He remembers each detail, from the plaster medallion accents to the Greco-Roman fireplaces to the twin-size window bench where he slept in the summer. "I remember everything about that house."[7] This Amplifier complements Smitherman's natural aptitudes, and it has supported his success and fulfillment in pursuing the building arts.

Adding It All Up

Numerical Computation allows you to quickly and accurately perform basic math in your head. You can whip up an annual budget with ease, and you automatically sense what you owe before the waiter brings the check. Making quick change at a tag sale, multiplying a recipe for a large party, and splitting the utility bill with your roommates all come naturally to you. While you may aggravate the department store clerk by pointing out their failure to grant the advertised 25 percent discount, your friends can trust you to be a reliable treasurer in Monopoly.

Though very different, Numerical Computation and Numerical Reasoning (described in the previous chapter) make a dynamic data duo. In 2014, Sam Cade began creating custom cakes for friends on a whim, using the kitchen of her University of Texas dorm. Her experimentation with cake decorating eventually led her into the realm of sugar art, and soon she was crafting strikingly realistic renditions of everything from cans of Bud Light to Rolex watches. Invited onto the popular Netflix show *Is It Cake?*, her work could fool even the most astute observers. Each cake order requires the creation of a one-of-a-kind confection, so Cade has to make constant mental calculations to price her work. "Every single cake is different—ingredients, amount of fondant, hours of work, even box size," she notes. "So, it's always quick mental math to determine the cost."

Carving a Nike shoe or a jar of Hellmann's mayonnaise from a stack of sheet cakes also produces a lot of excess icing and scraps, which Cade calls "Cake Guts." She sells these separately through Goldbelly, an online purveyor of fine foods. "My Numerical Reasoning skills have developed along with my bakery," she says. "My accountant helped me understand how to think about the numbers in order to reach profitability. And once I had the basics explained to me, it became a piece of cake!"[8]

Like Associative Memory, Numerical Computation gives you an advantage in traditional schooling as well. The test for this Amplifier only includes elementary math concepts, but the speed and accuracy of your answers indicate your level of ease and comfort in making the small yet vital computations of everyday life. Even if this Amplifier isn't part of your own internal wiring, you can still reach a reasonable level of competence by exercising your math muscle. For example, try solving a few simple equations in your head each morning without using a pencil, paper, or calculator. Then see whether you can walk or cook at the same time you are crunching numbers. This practice isn't just good for your confidence; it boosts your mental health, as well. Just one addition or subtraction problem can help to keep cognitive decline at bay.[9]

Show Me

Hand-Eye Coordination is a measure of how easily you translate visual or instructional cues delivered from a screen into body movements. If you receive a strong score in this Amplifier, you are a kinesthetic learner, meaning that you absorb information via physical activity. Whether you are taking an online yoga lesson, playing an instrument, navigating a new video game, learning to sew, or swinging a golf club, you can pick up new skills. The growing use of virtual reality training to help everyone from mechanics to surgeons learn new skills means that those with this aptitude are in luck. They can soak up new techniques like a sponge, locking in movements to support even the most complex tasks.

More Cherries

Beyond the assessment in this book, there are many other fascinating and highly specific aptitudes that can be measured if you have the time and inclination, but they aren't part of the YouScience assessment. Below are a few of the more interesting ones.

How's Your Ear?

The auditory amplifiers, also known as the musical aptitudes, relate to your ear for pitch and your ability to grasp and hold on to tone and rhythm. In the early twentieth century, Swedish psychologist Carl Seashore pioneered the testing of these specialized aptitudes. In 1919 he wrote *Seashore Measures of Musical Talents*, a title that might suggest the notes of a violin accompanied by lapping waves and seagulls. In fact, the book features five subtests aimed at measuring a person's sense of sound pitch, intensity, time, consonance, and tone (a 1925 revision added a sixth test for rhythm).

"Not all facets of musical aptitude are known," Seashore acknowledged, "but there are several fundamental capacities that can be assessed." The format of these tests changed over time and also adapted to shifts in American culture. For example, in the 1930s, the popularity of atonal music led to the replacement of the consonance test with a timbre measure. Subsequent studies in the 1960s revealed how environmental factors such as socioeconomic status, home life, musical interests and exposure had an impact on a person's test results. More recently, scientists have started to explore the impact of genetics and the brain's neurobiology on our personal sense of pitch (or lack thereof).[10]

"Some people can carry a tune," noted a wag named Richard Armour, "but they seem to stagger under the load." And while the Auditory Amplifiers can help to determine our "musical proclivity," they also point to a number of other latent capabilities.

Tonal Memory: How easily do you identify and remember sounds? Do you have a hard time getting a song out of your head? People with exceptional tonal memory can hear a song once and remember it forever. Those with this gift may find it easier to not just remember tunes, but, like *My Fair Lady*'s Professor Henry Higgins, they can accurately guess someone's hometown based on their accent, or pick up a language during a short trip abroad. They can pinpoint which birdsong belongs to the blue-winged warbler. You may have an ear for tune and love music, but you might not remember the exact pattern of notes in a song after you leave the concert. A friend with strong tonal memory will be humming it all week.

Rhythm Memory: This is a knack for remembering cadence and tempo. You might be that person who turns up the bass and taps your toe to the rhythm of a song, and you're a natural on the drums. Runners, equestrians, and even skilled orators have this Amplifier, which helps them rock to various beats in their daily lives. Great playwrights, poets, and public speakers know the importance of musicality in their work. The simplest explanation of iambic pentameter is the sound of our own heartbeats (da-DUM, da-DUM, da-DUM, one unstressed syllable followed by a stressed one), a rhythm Shakespeare used in his melodic lines (i.e., "to BE, or NOT, to BE").[11]

Pitch Discrimination: Some people have a keen ability to discern minuscule differences between sounds, an indication of near or perfect pitch. For better or worse, they have an expert's ear for the sour notes that come out of their own mouths or those of their choral neighbors. A few singers, such as Julie Andrews, Ella Fitzgerald, and Mariah Carey, personify this gift. Those who repair or tune musical instruments deploy it, though these days they can also use digital tuning apps as a backup.

The ability to discriminate between pitches also extends beyond the orbit of music. Indeed, being able to accurately distinguish between high and low sounds is associated with how precisely you discern minute differences in taste, smell, and sight. Have you ever tapped on a watermelon at the grocery store to test its ripeness? A dull thud indicates an overripe dampness in the fruit, telling you it is past its prime. To make Italy's renowned Parmigiano-Reggiano cheese, independent cheese experts (*battitore*) use pitch discrimination in their annual inspection of cheese quality. Using a small hammer, they tap, tap, tap around the entire wheel of cheese, listening for subtle variations in the sound. A consistent, even pitch means there are no holes or cavities inside the wheel, indicating superior quality. Uneven sounds point to possible defects caused by improper fermentation.

While many languages are tonal, nontonal languages rely on accurate pitch discrimination. A whistled language used on the island of La Gomera, in the Canary Islands, mimics Castilian Spanish and serves as a kind of public address system among islanders living in a mountainous terrain of peaks and vast canyons. Used to announce important news such as births and deaths, the language replaces each spoken vowel or consonant with a whistling sound. Users employ distinct whistles for just two vowels and four Spanish consonants, using subtle changes in undulation, pitch, and context to express full linguistic complexity.[12]

What's That Sound?

In the candlelit dining room of the Addams mansion, the wind howls and Lurch the butler plays a sinister tune on the organ as the family summons their uncle Fester from the dead. When Pugsley Addams pulls out a cleaver to threaten his sister Wednesday, the blade makes a menacing, prolonged *ting*. The background noises blend so seamlessly into the final film that we barely notice them. But in reality, each one was carefully selected and added during postproduction.

Known as Foley artists, the people who create this panoply of sound effects have a particular aptitude for discerning different types and pitches of noise. Interpreting the world primarily based on what they hear, rather than what they see or touch, they can distinguish varieties of *clang*, *squeak*, or *shhhh* sounds that most of us miss. They speak with their own vocabulary, scouring junkyards for "resonators," "ka-chunkers," and "sha-shonkers." They willingly experiment with even the most repulsive or outlandish objects, eager to see what noises might result. In order to create the sound that E.T. makes when he moves, two seasoned Foley artists used Jell-O encased in a damp T-shirt and a package of raw liver. The crinkle of Kate Winslet's hair frosting over as she floats among the wreckage of the *Titanic* is actually made by prying leaves of frozen lettuce away from their stem.

As film director David Lynch has noted, the best sound effects are the ones that resemble a kind of music. Foley artists have an acute awareness of sound pitch, tone, and texture that allows them to find just the right noises, evoking not only the reality but the *feeling* of a place or scene.[13]

Wow, You're Good!

The following aptitudes boost your performance at work, improve your stamina for certain related activities, or may just impress your friends.

Hue Discrimination: When you visit a paint store do all of the whites look the same, or can you easily discern between "marrow white," "dry-erase board white," and "trampled snow white"? Do you find yourself vacillating between the heather-gray sweater and the slate-gray one in your closet? Those with this aptitude see a complete and nuanced spectrum of colors. Interior designers, fashion consultants, and graphic designers are just a few professions that draw upon this remarkable ability.

Glare Factor: Do you reach for those aviator sunglasses each time you get in the car? This aptitude measures the tipping point at which glare impedes your vision. That may seem like a superfluous bit of information, but it can save lives if you happen to commute long distances or drive for a living. It can also be a boon for stage performers. If you are planning to train as a fighter pilot, be sure to get evaluated for this aptitude.

Finger Dexterity: Are you all thumbs, or are your hands your most essential tools? This aptitude determines how well you manipulate objects using your ten digits. Those who garden, knit, sculpt, strum, and massage make constant use of this aptitude. It can also come in "handy" when typing and texting.

Tweezer Dexterity: Do you find working with small tools easy or satisfying? Surgeons, dentists, jewelers, model hobbyists, and makeup artists rely heavily on this narrow but critical aptitude. With this Amplifier, you find it easy to thread a needle, hook a worm, apply makeup, and replace your watch battery. You're spared the expense of a salon when your eyebrows need plucking, and you reliably dominate the popular kid's game Operation. If you thrive when asked to perform under higher stakes, with training you could likely wield a scalpel with precision.

A Nose That Knows

Who knows what other innate super abilities you have yet to discover? Only recently scientists have discovered the health benefits of having a good nose. Ten years into marriage, Joy Milne noticed her husband Les's normal musky scent had turned into something more repugnant. She kindly nudged him to bathe more frequently, but hygiene wasn't the problem. When Les was later diagnosed with Parkinson's disease, Joy insisted she had smelled the worsening malady all along. Scientists were skeptical at first, but a Parkinson's specialist at the University of Edinburgh eventually decided it was worth investigating. He gave Joy a pile of T-shirts, each of which had been worn by a different person overnight, and asked her to use her nose to identify the shirts worn by someone with Parkinson's. She correctly picked out all the shirts worn by afflicted individuals, including one person who wasn't diagnosed with the disease until months after the experiment.[14]

The more we understand the awesome breadth of human potential, the greater our appreciation for the wonders of neurodiversity and how it can benefit our relationships and our achievements in business, medicine, education, and other fields. Still, these natural talents, alone, do not determine our course through life. Our aptitudes combine and manifest in extraordinary ways for each one of us, in large part because they are guided by our own unique personalities and interests.

Part IV

Personality and More

Distinct from your aptitudes, your personality characteristics are good indicators of the roles you gravitate toward, regardless of your chosen profession. To put it simply, aptitudes tell you where your *potential* lies, while personality concerns your *preferences*.

For example, your aptitude pattern may suggest that teaching would be a natural fit, but do you have a proclivity for diving deep into one subject, rather than rotating among many? After all, there is a big difference between a fourth-grade elementary teacher who presents a broad range of subjects to the class each day and a high school physics teacher who is devoted to a single discipline. While both are technically teachers, each one has a different Work Approach according to how they take on roles.

Another aspect of your personality, Interpersonal Style, has to do with extroversion and introversion. Do you revel in work environments where there is constant social interplay? Do you feel best working alone, or in the company of a smaller group? This important facet of our personalities helps us to understand what, exactly, energizes us and why. Some go into medicine because they enjoy delivering direct care to patients, drawing vitality from their interactions, while others choose to do medical research, invigorated by solo work. Understanding your unique combination of Work Approach and Interpersonal Style will help you target roles where you can flourish.

Finally, we end this book with a word about putting your talents to work once you've identified them. Whether you're just starting out on your career path, in the middle of it, or nearing the end of the journey, your hidden genius demands expression. Someday, you may retire, but it will not. This guide will help you every step along the way.

CHAPTER 9

Work Approach and Interpersonal Style

The fox knows many things; the hedgehog one big thing.
—Archilochus

WORK APPROACH

Specialist   ❰ ❰ ❰ ❰ ❰   Liaison   ❱ ❱ ❱ ❱ ❱   Generalist

One of Apple TV's favorite characters, Ted Lasso (played by Jason Sudeikis), doesn't know a thing about the game of soccer when he's recruited to coach the English team, AFC Richmond. The intimidating new team owner, Rebecca, takes over control after a nasty divorce, and she initially hires this Midwestern college football coach to sabotage her ex-husband's beloved team. To her surprise, Ted Lasso proves to be an equally effective coach despite his total ignorance of the game. Relying on relationship-building, motivational pep talks, and good humor—along with an unshakable dedication to the motto "believe"—Lasso lets his soccer stars shine individually by bringing them together to become a unified whole. Lasso knows that his success is in the team's success, and the team's success comes down to each individual member. "If you just figure out a way to turn that 'me' into 'us,'" he lectures to one of the more egotistical, but talented players, Jamie, "the sky's the limit for you."[1] His tireless commitment to a bunch of players who possess peak athletic ability but lack the requisite camaraderie for winning eventually leads to a collective power that proves infallible.

Lasso's lack of knowledge and experience doesn't preclude him from being an effective coach, because he is open to learning and ever willing to stay flexible.

What kind of person can devote himself so completely to shared success? Who is capable of letting the experts shine precisely because he isn't trying to be an expert? How could someone like Jamie become a better player—and person—with the help of someone like Lasso?

It turns out that Lasso and his team have a symbiotic relationship that isn't entirely unique to this fictional comedy show. It's a relationship created by complementary personality traits.

What's Your Work Approach?

Are you a Generalist who gravitates toward projects that allow you to collaborate and work with others to achieve a common goal? Do you command knowledge across a wide swath of subjects, but don't necessarily have specific expertise? Many Generalists crave variety in their work, and they relish the chance to jump in and play pinch hitter when doing so advances a shared objective. They comprise the bulk of the population (about 75 percent), and typically develop broad skill sets that can be applied across diverse situations.

While the wide-angle camera lens used by Generalists facilitates objectivity, the 300mm zoom of the Specialists and Liaisons encourages subjectivity and requires more autonomy. Those at the left end of the

Work Approach continuum are invaluable team members, especially if they are given a wide berth and authority on the topics that interest them. Their hallmark is diving deep and sharing this specialized knowledge. Combined, Specialists and Liaisons make up only about 25 percent of the population, and often settle into the role of resident expert. (The Work Approach of Liaisons and Specialists is so similar that this chapter addresses them together.)

The YouScience assessment measures your Work Approach by giving you word prompts and asking you to respond with the first word that comes to mind. Generalists typically write in words that come automatically for most people. For example, if the prompt says "sky," a Generalist answers "blue," or "cloud," and so on, while a Specialist/Liaison could respond with something more unusual, like "cerulean" or "constellation."

Generalists like Ted Lasso tend to wear many different hats, and they excel at facilitating, managing, and collaborating with others in service of organizational goals. They embrace roles as team leaders, coaches, managers, and cheerleaders. When working in their element, Generalists will create generous space for the Specialists to do what they were born to do—play soccer, perform on-screen, write the novel, dance in front of the camera, run their lab experiments, or sculpt their clay. Natural delegators, Generalists thrive in situations where they can commission high-performing experts to help them execute a plan. Well-known Generalists include *Saturday Night Live* producer Lorne Michaels; American Red Cross CEO Gail McGovern; and Mary Barra, the head of General Motors.

Specialists and Liaisons, on the other hand, see their work as an extension of themselves. Unlike Generalists who easily pivot from one project or topic to the next, they are most comfortable and effective as experts in their fields, and they seek out endeavors that will bear the mark of their own unique talents. For example, a Specialist working for a leisure travel company might carve out a niche for themselves by becoming the go-to authority on Bogotá, Colombia, thus creating a subspecialty beyond the more routine bookings he makes for Disney World and Las Vegas weekends.

If this personality trait describes you, you likely prefer to work independently or alone, and you are a key contributor to your teams, especially when you have complete control or ownership over your assignment. Because of your competence and expertise, you may be tapped for leadership roles, which can be a double-edged sword for some. Balancing the practice of your craft with the burden of managing others is a challenge not all Specialists embrace. (We'd be willing to place a handsome bet that *Vogue*'s longtime creative director, Grace Coddington, cellist Yo-Yo Ma, New York Philharmonic concertmaster Frank Huang, and Apple cofounder, Steve Wozniak would all score as Specialists.)

From Pink Slip to White House

Ronald Reagan's path to the presidency was anything but straight. Before becoming the leader of the free world, he was cast in a number of other roles. While most people know that he once worked as an actor, he only landed in Hollywood after stints as a lifeguard, radio announcer, journalist, and custodian for the women's dormitory at Eureka College.

Likewise, Blair Downing never imagined that his own meandering career path would land him in the White House as it did in 2021. In 1985, after four years working for Vanderbilt University, twenty-five-year-old Downing was eager to move to Washington, DC, and participate in national politics. With the help of a mentor, he secured a series of political appointments, the most significant of which was an administrative position with the Treasury Department. During his eight years there he learned to navigate the complicated hive of offices that are situated to the east of the executive residence. He discovered his knack for managing the flow of information and coordinating among various stakeholders, and he came to feel valued among his co-workers as an indispensable asset. "I gained a reputation for being good at putting together briefing books and circulating them," he recalls. "One of my habits was to deliver materials by way of the third floor, where the secretary of the treasury, undersecretaries, and associated staff had their offices, so I could connect with everyone."

Four years later, when Bill Clinton was elected, the new administration issued pink slips to most political appointees—including Downing, who found himself standing at a career crossroads. "I had six weeks of paid leave. But it ended up that I was unemployed for a year and a half, or maybe longer than that," he recalls. "I created a lot of worry for my mother and my partner . . . but to be honest, I had a perfectly good time." Downing was dabbling in a series of odd jobs when a friend asked him to help run an event rental business at an iconic historic property, Evermay. Building on his years of orchestrating undersecretaries and policy wonks within the maze of the executive branch, Downing fell easily into his new role. Each wedding or corporate event involved coordinating multiple vendors including caterers, florists, musicians, rentals, audio-video contractors, and parking valets. The work felt like a natural extension of his old job, albeit in a completely different arena.

As his reputation as a skilled manager grew, Susan Gage, owner of a bespoke catering service, tapped him to lead two of her premier accounts, Georgetown University and the official residence of the vice president at Number One Observatory Circle. "I did everything from a small lunch for the king of Jordan to a party for Prince Charles," he remembers. "And so, during that period, I worked for three vice presidential families, the Bushes, the Bidens, and the Pences.

"Then, in the fall of 2021, I got this call from Anthony Bernal, senior adviser to the First Lady," he told us. "He asked if I would consider taking over the job of chief usher," meaning Chief Usher of the White House. Downing said yes.

Like the connective tissue between independent muscles, Downing makes sure the varied and ever-complicated collaborations among housekeepers, butlers, chefs, calligraphers, engineers, plumbers, electricians, curators, and others work seamlessly. The position is not political, and for Downing, it isn't personal, either. As a true Generalist, his mission at work remains separate from his identity. His main objective is to serve the president and the First Family, and to provide "the institution—and the people that work there—the resources to do their jobs and to make sure they understand what is expected."[2]

In this multifaceted role, no two days are the same. He doesn't need to know how to perform every job, but he is thoroughly familiar with the standards required of each expert on the team and their contribution to the smooth operation of the "People's House" in a way that reflects the ideals of the United States.

The Generalist

Downing told us how, in his first months on the job at the White House, he made no attempt at changes. Instead, he spent his time listening, observing, supporting, and trying not to interfere in the work of the individual experts that made up his team. Regardless of whether or not they fill a managerial role, all Generalists are truly "go along to get along" people. They prioritize shared wins over individual victories. They're comfortable giving as well as taking directions, leading and following, listening and talking.

Generalists' broad perspectives also help them to recognize when to let go. Rather than stubbornly clinging to an idea, plan, or project when it's clearly doomed, they readily take stock, regroup, and shift their focus according to input from trusted advisers and team members. They are also quick to collaborate with all the right authorities and experts.

Delegation is something Generalists take seriously, and they are particularly astute at matching talent with tasks. They readily defer to another team member when their skill in an area is outmatched, especially if this will enhance a project. For the Generalist, this realization isn't threatening, it's liberating. As the former General Electric CEO Jack Welch famously remarked, "Before you are a leader, success is all about growing yourself. When you become a leader, success is all about growing others."

Celebrity chef and entrepreneur Carla Hall is the first to acknowledge that her success would be impossible without her capable team. She relies on these "doers" who are committed to executing her many projects. Hall also credits the expertise of her talented assistant, who is a former business owner, for teaching her how to have an assistant. Learning to trust others, and resist any urge to micromanage, brings not only relief but freedom. For Hall, the creative juices can flow with the knowledge that others are both executing her vision and anticipating issues that might arise in the future.

Generalist Challenges

While Generalists can become superb managers, it can take years to accumulate the experience and expertise required for a leadership position. This means that you will likely need to develop some mastery in a given area first, which can be frustrating if you are young and, like a butterfly, flit from thing to thing. But think of your youthful years as valuable training that will help you to earn respect, become more discerning, and fully appreciate the contributions of each team member.

Many Generalists climb the corporate ranks through legal, marketing, or finance departments, where they spend years performing specialized functions. Plant managers, for instance, become familiar with all types of equipment, machines, and processes through experience before they are given the responsibility of leading a team of operators. Long before he became a legendary football coach, the Chicago Bears' Mike Ditka learned the game as a player.

Generalists might become annoyed if they find they are unable to delegate tasks, or if they feel that their colleagues aren't pulling their own weight. Disorderly workplaces and organizational systems, unclear management directions, and insufficiently trained or under-resourced staff are particularly exasperating for them. If left unchecked, these environments can cause Generalists to become exacting and sometimes impatient supervisors because, from their wide-angle view, honoring one's commitment and fully contributing to the team is paramount. Over time and with enough managerial experience, however, they can learn to overcome such pitfalls.

Dog trainer Marcus Wright navigates this challenge by focusing on communication. "I don't ever want to talk *at* people," he explained. "I really try to make sure that it's a two-way line of communication, and that the interns and trainers who work with me feel heard. And even if I know that what they're doing is not the most effective way to go about dealing with certain dog behaviors, we're still going to talk about it." As he confessed, "the hardest part of my job is managing personalities."[3]

A Taste of Joy

When the majority of us look at a map of Italy, we see an old-fashioned boot. The upper cuff consists of Genoa, Milan, and Venice, while midway down is the capital, Rome. Naples sits on the ankle, and Aspromonte National Park is part of the toe, kicking Sicily like a ball. A typical Generalist might see this map as a simple collection of cities and landmarks configured within the geographic contours of a piece of footwear. But when the sommelier Olivia Mason, a Specialist among Specialists, looks at the same map, she perceives—and almost tastes—a patchwork of regions known for their distinct wines.

Mason sees Piedmont in the north, home of two renowned red wines, the robust Barolo and the rich, spicy Barbaresco. Moving south into the foot, she finds Puglia and Calabria, both known for their own unique varieties of red wine. Sicily, a wine region that stands apart from the rest of the south, contains twenty-three subregions, or controlled domains of origin (*denominazione di origine controllata*), for the production of specific wines. "There are vast differences between north and south," she notes. "One sommelier might be an authority on northern Italian wines but know very little about the southern region. In my field, you need people who understand them separately."

As a Specialist, Mason doesn't just want to be an expert in wine. She seeks to be a connoisseur of the unique wines of the Piedmont region. A desire for intense expertise drives people like her to spend years pursuing formal certifications, credentials, diplomas, and training. Working her way through each varietal, Mason has tirelessly sharpened her tasting skills with reference to this single area of Italy.

She began her journey with a bachelor's degree in communications. After completing coursework in a specialized certification program, she passed a daylong test that earned her the title of certified sommelier. To deepen her understanding of wine and the businesses surrounding it, she then earned a diploma from the Wine & Spirit Education Trust. When we last spoke, she was completing the Italian Wine Scholar certification course, the most advanced Italian wine program available. In 2022, in recognition of her deep knowledge and expertise, she had the rare privilege of serving as a judge at the annual Decanter World Wine Awards in London.

Mason also writes articles filled with detailed and engaging descriptions of wines, features on lesser-known varieties, and interviews with legendary enologists for *Decanter* magazine. This and other varied roles within her métier have brought her enormous fulfillment, matching her Specialist personality. As she commented, "I've realized just how much autonomy I have, and I find I want to do things myself."[4]

The Specialists/Liaisons

When you were a young child, did you love to collect facts or objects— dinosaurs, baseball stats, Pokémon cards, stickers, or digital goods? As a teenage fan, did you consume every relevant book, website, or resource to learn more about your sports or music idol? And while this unusual degree of intensity felt normal to you, did you wonder why others didn't share your enthusiasm? It might have taken you time to fit in with a particular social group because you presumed that others shared your independent and deeply inquisitive mindset.

If you are a Specialist or a Liaison, you take your work very personally and prefer to have full ownership of your projects. Each time you craft a unique product or service, you glean subjective rewards. You enjoy being the point of reference for others, and you take pride in making unique or remarkable contributions. Self-employment may appeal to you, in part because you enjoy relying on your personal competence to muscle through challenges. You embrace opportunities that allow you to share your expert point of view, and you can be particularly well suited to roles that require you to provide consulting, advising, and mentoring to others.

After working as a high school teacher and coach, Specialist Brent Hull reached a point where, he says, he "wore too many hats." He decided to enroll in the North Bennet Street School's historic preservation program. Hull didn't just want to learn the building trade. He yearned to be a master craftsman. Based in Boston, Massachusetts, the narrowly focused, intensive program fit Hull's Specialist personality like the joint of a mortise and tenon. He soaked up each course, learning traditional millwork techniques, specific molding profiles, and near-extinct methods of construction.

After graduating, he founded Hull Works, a building company that offers a range of niche products and services. A self-described "museum-quality purist," Hull has become a sought-after builder known for his commitment to authenticity. "I do my work exactly the way it used to be done a hundred-plus years ago, all with the same hand tools and methods as when the building was originally made," he explains.[5]

In this line of work, Hull has found his way back to teaching, though not in the traditional sense. When the History Channel asked him to host the reality show *Lone Star Restoration* in 2016, he seized the opportunity to become a subject matter expert in the public eye, sharing his deep reservoir of knowledge with others. (While Specialists pour themselves wholeheartedly into what they love doing, they can also pursue more than one interest at a time.)

Specialist/Liaison Challenges

If you are a Specialist or a Liaison, you probably don't give yourself credit for knowing as much as you do. When you are thoroughly immersed in a subject, it can be easy to focus only on how much remains to be learned, at the cost of recognizing just how far you've come. Well accustomed to being the "go-to" person for your expertise, you can sometimes take offense when you are not consulted.

Viewing your work as a representation of yourself also makes you susceptible to perfectionism, and you may find it challenging or even heartbreaking to let go of something in which you've invested your time and energy. As difficult as it is to acknowledge when it's time to move on, listening to others can help you identify these pivotal moments and remain agile.

Still, it is important to recognize that such transitions can come with a real sense of mourning, as Olivia Mason discovered in middle school when she decided to quit competitive dance. Reflecting on that time in her life, Mason remembers how doing this "was a sad decision, but at the same time a really good one."[6] The turning point came when she realized that all the time she was putting into dance didn't make sense, because she didn't plan to pursue it professionally.

Interpersonal Style

Solitude matters, and for some people, it's the air they breathe.

—Susan Cain

INTERPERSONAL STYLE

Introvert   ⟨ ⟨ ⟨ ⟨ ⟨   Blended
Energizer   ⟩ ⟩ ⟩ ⟩ ⟩   Extrovert

Are you an Extrovert, an Introvert, or a little of both (what You-Science calls a "Blended Energizer")? The answer affects whether you'll enjoy outward-facing, highly interactive roles, or other positions that are less reliant on interfacing with colleagues and customers. Do you enjoy working remotely, or does doing so take an emotional toll? Do you like sharing what you know in front of a live audience, or do you prefer writing about it from the comfort of your office? Do you glean energy and inspiration from smaller, nimbler teams, or larger, more dynamic ones?

If you score as a Blended Energizer, your flexible nature and versatility tell others that you are "easygoing." You are just as content leading as following, stepping up, or backing off. You may have found yourself relating to different aspects of the Extrovert and the Introvert. We suggest you draw wisdom from both and use this adaptability to your advantage.

While it's easy to think that there is a natural link between Specialists and Liaisons and Introverts on one hand, and Generalists and Extroverts on the other, these two personality trait continuums are not two parallel lines; rather, they more closely resemble a tangled, fuzzy knot. While Extroverted Specialists particularly enjoy sharing their insights with others, Introverted Specialists prefer to make their work available through publishing, consulting, or other, behind-the-scenes means, independent of direct, larger-scale public interaction.

Extroverted Specialist Brent Hull could never have found fulfillment in building custom marquetry tables in a workshop by himself. Instead, being able to impart his knowledge and expertise to an attentive audience through television, blogs, and teaching opportunities has brought him enormous satisfaction. "I love encouraging young people to care as much as I do about building good things," he says.[7] Carla Hall, another Extroverted Specialist, also draws an audience wherever she goes. Her enthusiasm for the culinary arts inspires even the most timid cooks to don an apron and fire up the stove.

Introverted Specialists don't need the sound of applause in order to feel energized and motivated; they prefer to reveal themselves through their words, art, or discoveries. For example, Lutheran seminarian Jonas Sorensen drew an audience of 72,000 strangers to his spirituality blog, earning it the title of "top single-author publication" on *Medium* in 2015. His writings on living a more spiritual life have been shared with thousands and spread through extensive social networks from the solitude of his home. "It's amazing how many people you can reach beyond a single, confined congregation," he observed. "While I love sharing my words with people in the pews, I am equally excited about sharing them with readers I've never met."[8]

Extroverted Generalists such as Blair Downing seek the satisfying buzz of linking together people and ideas. They bounce from group to group, person to person, finding points of synergy and mutual areas of interest. The success of their team or family is their *raison d'être*, and the group's achievements feel like their own. As Downing has said, he "wants everybody to be happy." But he also notes how "personnel management is one of the hardest parts of my job as chief usher. There are 85 people and 104 personalities," he laughs.[9] Downing lives for this team and for the fulfillment he finds in rising to meet the challenge of managing them.

Introverted Generalists tap into similar motivations, but operate best when they are able to exchange ideas one-on-one. They view collaboration as a series of small group dialogues and work teams. They enjoy coming to the office, but they keep the small conference room on permanent reserve.

It might surprise you to learn that many CEOs are self-described Introverts. They focus primarily on the value of delivering patient nurturing, coaching, and mentoring to each individual member of their teams. Douglas Conant, the much-loved former CEO of Campbell's Soup, found success in "building alliances one person at a time." As Susan Cain notes on her blog, *Quiet Revolution*, Conant "wrote over *thirty thousand* handwritten letters to thank employees for a job well done." In leading thousands, Conant viewed his job as rooted in one-on-one relationships.[10]

We have highlighted the extremes here, as examples, but it is rare to find someone who is purely an Extrovert or an Introvert. Like the aptitudes and your Work Approach, Interpersonal Style moves along a continuum, and your score can vary depending on the circumstances of your life, family, and work. Either way, knowing whether you see the world with a more objective or subjective bent, and what kinds of activities will energize or sap you, will help you to filter out certain roles within a profession, nudging you toward a better work fit than what your aptitudes or interests alone might suggest.

Personal Values, Goals, and Circumstances

At this point, you may be thinking, "What about everything beyond my aptitude, interests, and personality profiles? There are lots of other things I need to consider when managing my career!" You are absolutely right. Our personal values, goals, and circumstances all influence the kinds of jobs and the types of roles we pursue.

Perhaps you don't feel true satisfaction until you get your hands dirty and see the tangible results of your efforts, or maybe you need to know—above all else—that your work is directly improving the lives of others. Many fields can satisfy both of these objectives, but understanding your own values and goals will help you navigate your way to a more rewarding position within those domains. Whether you prefer the more physical work of a wildland firefighter, or the investigative tasks associated with being an environmental restoration planner, both careers protect our natural resources. When volunteering for your favorite nonprofit organization, do you want to see the faces you're serving and work directly with the people the group aims to help, or are you happier explaining the cause to wealthy donors who can support it? Your answer to this question can help steer you toward roles that fulfill you.

At some point in your life, you've likely contemplated some enticing option that ultimately didn't align with your values. Money or security might have been handed to you like a shiny package, but your priorities prevented you from accepting. Maybe you've been offered your ideal job, but the commute would mean spending two fewer hours each day with your kids. What if a higher-paying job pops up on LinkedIn that aligns perfectly with your college major, but the company is a known supporter of a cause you abhor? Does what you value trump what you might gain in terms of monetary and career advancement? We face tough dilemmas like these all the time, and there are always trade-offs. Nothing is ever all good or all bad.

Take Tracy Crowley, for example. A seasoned teacher, she has worked her way up through the ranks to the role of curriculum developer and teacher trainer. Now in her forties, she makes a handsome salary. But over time, she has found the work less and less fulfilling. Still, she's clear about her values: time with family, travel, and fun side projects with nonprofits. Understanding that her job allows her to do all of these things, she uses her spacious teacher's schedule to do adventurous gigs for *National Geographic*; she goes to a new country every school break; she develops her photography skills.

And what about the goals you've been setting for yourself, all your life? Are you motivated by a future you can't yet see? Or do you prefer to fix your eyes on goals whose finish lines are in clear sight? An analogy from the sport of track and field helps here. Track and field features a whole host of events, and each one requires a different training regimen. Some people are sprinters, blasting forward with everything they've got and reaching the tape within seconds, totally spent. Others are built for the long haul of a marathon, their measured paces and steady breathing calculated to preserve their energy over a grueling twenty-six miles. Each runner finds the event that suits their pace, but they all share the same goal of crossing the finish line.

While some are content to work years toward a goal without any immediate reward, others work best with short-term deadlines that help keep them focused and motivated. Knowing what kinds of goals you like to set can guide you toward jobs that match your aspirational perspective. Your Time Frame Orientation measure in YouScience will also give you some idea.

Other critical factors to consider have to do with things you can't necessarily control on your own—your current phase in life, your general economic and environmental conditions, your personal and family's health, and so on. Your personal circumstances have a sizable influence on not just the opportunities afforded you, but the decisions you make. The good news is that whatever jobs happen to disappear or emerge in the future, you can be sure they will need not just a range of aptitude and interest profiles, but Generalists, Specialists, Extroverts, Introverts, and every personality in between.

Regardless of where you are in life, your newly discovered assets will surely set a course for some uncharted territory. So hold on tight. The surprising places you're headed will be exactly right for you.

CHAPTER 10

Setting a Course

We shall not cease from exploration
And the end of all our exploring
Will be to arrive where we started
And know the place for the first time.
—T. S. Eliot

In June 1997, English speakers around the world first met the sorting hat at Hogwarts School for Witchcraft and Wizardry. When placed upon a nervous pupil's head, it would make a decision about which "house" the child should be in and shout "Gryffindor!" or "Slytherin!" to enthusiastic cheers. This miraculous sorting ritual required nothing of the young witch or wizard, other than to sit quietly and wait; no test, no survey, no interview. Yet the wrinkly brown hat with a mouth unfailingly landed on the right choice.

For centuries, humans have sorted themselves in novel ways in an effort to make sense of a chaotic, nonsensical world. The ever-popular zodiac system first emerged around 2,500 years ago in Babylonia, and numerology dates back to 500 BCE. Even today, many people scrutinize the stars, number patterns, and birthdates to categorize themselves and others, or for some hint of the future. And despite the many scientific and technological breakthroughs of the modern era, our understanding of ourselves and our potential remains in the early innings of a very long game.

As you've learned in this book, the aptitude-based assessments of today reveal the most critical parts of what make you, you. Grounded in science rather than, say, phrenology or astrology, they at last offer a more accurate picture of who you are and where you might go. With the help of aptitude assessment tools, you can better understand the source of your greatest proclivities, motivations, and habits. Your assessment results explain why your boss or partner irritates you, why you keep avoiding risk, why you feel restless, or why selecting the best bananas at the grocery store always brightens your day. For most, this deeper comprehension validates aspects of themselves that they already knew intuitively but could never articulate, like a song that perfectly captures all our scattered thoughts and feelings about ourselves and the world. Best of all, the confidence you gain from this new understanding of your natural abilities will propel you toward greater exploration and growth.

The O*NET Edge

If we could create an adult sorting hat for careers, what would it look like? The Occupational Information Network (O*NET) comes pretty close. The YouScience assessment gives you unlimited access to a personalized career dashboard powered by O*NET, the United States' primary database of job types. Using your YouScience results, the O*NET search engine draws upon its massive store of career data to suggest the jobs most suitable to your aptitudes, interests, and personality.

Although job analysis experts first standardized O*NET's occupation descriptors in the 1990s, the information and the algorithms used to manipulate it are regularly updated and maintained to keep pace with the changing job market. A dedicated team of seasoned industrial and organizational psychologists tracks diverse skills and occupations in real time, as they continue to shift with advances in digital technology and the workplace.

Still, because of the rapid pace of the changing job market, the information will always lag a bit. Further, some categories, such as work in the spiritual fields, are absent. We encourage you to keep this in mind and view the career suggestions as take-off points rather than literal prescriptions.

While portions of O*NET data have been used to match people with occupations for decades, this powerful resource has not been utilized to its fullest extent. Just as we improve our internet searches by typing in descriptive keywords, we can optimize our occupational "fit" matches when we input better data. Thus, when the input is limited to interest survey responses, the output is an overwhelming number of career suggestions. But insert more detailed data, such as interests plus aptitudes, and the results are far more refined. You can find this personalized information in your YouScience career dashboard.

Powered by O*NET's robust store of data, your YouScience career dashboard uses your aptitudes, interests, and personality traits to showcase opportunities. Some of the recommendations will surprise you. Much like the case with Netflix's algorithm-driven entertainment suggestions and the personalized dating recommendations generated by Hinge or other apps, what you do with the information is entirely up to you. If an intriguing or unusual occupation appears on your shortlist, take some time to learn more and explore your potential options. And remember, if you do decide to set off in a new direction, you may need to develop your existing aptitudes and cultivate the skills required to make your dream job a reality.

Many of your career recommendations will not only differ starkly from one another, they may challenge your own vision for what you thought you wanted to do, or deviate significantly from what you've been doing for the past thirty years. For example, you might currently work in marketing, but many of your "best career fits" include the word *engineer*. This kind of revelation can lead to doubt, bewilderment, and a fair amount of soul-searching. Some practical questions may prove distracting: *How am I going to afford all that additional schooling? When will I find the time? What if we have to move so I can get the right training? How will I support myself while I'm learning?*

These questions are normal, so if you start to feel overwhelmed, we recommend you let things "settle." Don't do anything right away. You don't need to quit your job immediately and return to school. Instead, spend some time learning more about your options online. Think about how you might, for example, transfer your marketing skills to industries that will allow you to work with engineers. Just a few small changes at work and at home can lead to enormous improvements in your satisfaction and use of your aptitudes.

Above all, the changes you make in reaction to your newly discovered hidden genius will depend on where you are in life. What are your circumstances? How old are you? Do you feel financially secure? And where do you stand in terms of your aspirations? Are you still reaching toward an ideal or a particular profession, or are you seeking ways to dial back?

From a career standpoint, our lives unfold in three broad stages: our late teens and twenties (the Exploratory stage), the thirties and forties (the Building stage), and the fifties and beyond (the Pro stage). There are no set boundaries between these stages or rules dictating when you will pass through them. The central themes of each stage also overlap, because people in their fifties can still explore, and those in their thirties are already skilled in various ways. Life is, well, life, and each of our paths is entirely unique. Just ask that stranger sitting next to you on the plane what they do for a living, and how they got there (chances are, it may be a long story!). Nonetheless, splitting these diverse life trajectories into three rough stages can help us step back and appreciate how our skills and priorities shift over time, and how we can use that perspective to shape our futures.

The Explorers

Psychologist Meg Jay describes our twenties as "the defining decade" of our lives, or "a developmental sweet spot: a time when the things we do—and the things we don't do—will have an enormous impact across years and even generations to come."[1] In this Exploratory stage, many of us face a dizzying array of choices. Should we go to college? What about graduate school? Is it wise to give our dreams a try even if it means living hand-to-mouth, or would that just put off the necessity of having a job that pays the bills? Should we travel before "settling down"? In this stage of life, many of us date and find a mate. We might have children. We could be choosing where to live, even if we end up moving later in life. We start to decide what kinds of financial risks we are willing to take.

This is also the stage in which most of us leave our childhood nests and find a way to start supporting ourselves. We make critical choices about our priorities and who we want to be as adults. Our species likes to sleep indoors, and preferably not on our parents' couches, so money is a primary motivator that can paralyze, panic, or focus us. While some young people choose to follow prescriptive training regimens (in the military, academia, or medicine, for example), the majority spend these years exploring their options. Today's college graduates will change jobs (and even industries) an average of four times before they reach the age of thirty-two.[2]

If you are in the Exploratory stage, you can take a long-term perspective that will allow you to stay agile as you navigate your future. Your greatest allies at this point are time and your ability to be versatile. More than at other stages of life, you can glean the greatest benefit from exploring jobs that align most closely with your aptitudes.

Although subjective interest inventories can be appealing and tantalizingly accessible, they can also distract and even harm young people considering their career possibilities. Particularly in the Exploratory stage, factors like our upbringing, economic circumstances, and peer groups make us particularly prone to following our passions of the moment, rather than our unique skills, expertise, or work experience. But pursuing our interests can short-change our career potential, while social and cultural biases can lead to damaging mismatches between our aptitudes and interests.

For instance, this effect contributes to the underrepresentation of women and minorities in roles traditionally occupied by white men. It helps to explain why the interest inventory results for high school females have indicated a weak fit for STEM fields, despite a close alignment between their aptitudes and the skills required by STEM careers (which often match as well or even better than with their male peers' aptitudes).[3] One 2020 study conducted by the University of Missouri and YouScience was designed to examine the lack of women in science, technology, engineering, and mathematics—a.k.a. "STEM"—fields. The researchers distributed aptitude assessments and career-interest surveys to 7,200 students in fourteen states and compared the students' aptitude results with their self-reported interest in jobs in manufacturing, technology, construction, and healthcare. They found significant discrepancies in the male and female students' interests: 39 percent of boys expressed interest in computer technology jobs, compared with 12 percent of girls; 31 percent of girls expressed interest in healthcare jobs that involve caring for patients, compared with 19 percent of boys.

But their aptitude scores told a different story. Not only did 26 percent of girls demonstrate a high aptitude fit for computer technology; they outscored the boys by four percentage points. At the same time, boys' aptitude scores indicated that 23 percent of them would be a good fit for the patient-care jobs in which they hadn't expressed as much interest.[4]

The YouScience career dashboard allows you to step beyond your interests and explore how other aspects of yourself might complement specific jobs. As you peruse your career recommendations, it is important to filter your results by not only "interest fit," but also by "aptitude fit" and "overall fit," which also takes your personality into account. While your interests can help to guide you throughout your life, don't forget that your fascination with certain things may fade with time.

This is why interest inventories can only capture your perspective at a single point in your life, effectively inviting you to miss the forest for the trees. Your friends' hobbies; the professions of your parents or relatives; even the TV show you watched last night can influence your survey answers.[5] True, the results of an interest survey represent whatever appeals to you right now. But they fail to capture the full range of options you *might* explore. And even if your current activities align with both your aptitudes and your interests, careers are in a constant state of flux. Knowing your enduring natural talents allows you to nimbly respond to a shifting career landscape. No one knows this more than a child sports prodigy. You probably know one—or maybe you were one—and they're an enviable anomaly.

Ready for a Curveball

Often athletes' talents are so celebrated it's hard for them to imagine doing anything else; they become inextricably linked to their sport, and for some, the rewards for their commitment are significant. But with only 2 percent of high school athletes (1 in 57) going on to play for NCAA Division I schools, and of these only 2 percent continuing to the professional level, it is easy to see that a career in competitive sports is, by design, short-lived. Even if they do become part of this 2 percent, consider the fact that the median age of an Olympic athlete is just twenty-five years old. The stats may dissuade some, but competitive athletes are wired differently. Despite the numbers and the inevitability of an early, forced retirement, they go for the gold anyway.

Thirty-four-year-old Stacie Townsend knows this well. From the age of nine, competitive softball was her number one priority. Her determination and command on the pitcher's mound propelled her to the highest brackets of the sport including a spot on the Great Britain National Softball team. "As a kid, I never had much of a plan past making the Olympics," she says. She describes this extreme kind of focus as "tunnel vision." Sure, she knew all professional athletes face an earlier expiration date than other professionals, but she didn't let the thought of what would come next distract her from her goal. Even when softball was officially cut from the Olympic Games in 2009, Townsend stayed the course through college, holding on to hopes that an appeal might reinstate the sport while she was still competing.

When it became clear that her Olympic dreams would never materialize, Townsend faced the same uncertainty and feelings of obsolescence typically associated with those later in life. With the support of a family friend and mentor, she came to realize that while her athletic prowess was always her most obvious gift, it was really only one notch on a very long belt of talents. Her aptitudes for Visual Scanning and

Diagnostic Problem-Solving were applicable on the ballfield but easily redeployed in an entirely new arena, the field of law. Today she is a corporate attorney for Gunster law firm in Florida.

What Will They Think?

In the 1990s, a team of researchers asked college students to walk alone into a social setting wearing a T-shirt emblazoned with the face of the eighties pop star Barry Manilow, a mortifying fashion choice at the time. Asked to estimate how others in the room would react, the students guessed that 50 percent would notice their awful taste in shirts. In fact, only 25 percent did. In a follow-up study, participants wore shirts bearing the face of someone more generally admired—Bob Marley, Jerry Seinfeld, or Martin Luther King Jr. Again, they guessed that 50 percent of the other people would notice their fashion choices. Only 10 percent did.[6]

When we are in our twenties and thirties, we're highly self-conscious and many of us worry about what others could be thinking or saying about us. But in reality, people aren't paying much attention. Psychologists call this "the spotlight effect."

Once, at a professional event, Betsy ran into a friend of hers—someone with whom she had interacted several times in the past. She assumed that this person would at least know the basics of what was going on in her life, even though they didn't keep in regular touch. But when she mentioned the name of the company she was working for at the time (following many years spent raising children), he looked at her in surprise.

"Oh! I didn't realize you were back at work. How long have you been there?"

"Eight years," she said, with a laugh.

At that moment, she knew she could either be hurt that he didn't have a clue about her change in circumstances, or she could gracefully accept the fact that, quite simply, he hadn't been paying attention. She chose the latter, which prompted a liberating realization: *No one cares.*

Too often, we're prevented from making important life decisions because we're worried about what people might think. These flawed assumptions are ready fodder for the kind of rationalizing that leads to poor decisions. So, we suggest reframing the narrative by de-prioritizing the concerns of others. For example:

"IF I DON'T GO TO HARVARD LAW AND INSTEAD CHOOSE TO PURSUE MY ART, MY FAMILY WILL BE DISAPPOINTED."	*COULD BE:*	"IF I GO TO HARVARD LAW WHEN I'M NOT PASSIONATE ABOUT OR BUILT FOR LAW, I'M THE ONE WHO WILL CARRY THE DEBT AND REGRET."
"IF I DECIDE NOT TO MARRY, I'LL BE THE ONLY ONE OF MY FRIENDS WHO IS SINGLE."	*COULD BE:*	"IF I DECIDE NOT TO MARRY, I'LL BE BUILDING A LIFE THAT SUITS ME, AND I'M THE ONE WHO ULTIMATELY OWNS THAT CHOICE."
"IF I GO BACK TO WORK AFTER STAYING HOME WITH MY SON FOR SO LONG, MY FRIENDS WILL ALL BE WAY MORE ADVANCED IN THEIR CAREERS. I'LL FEEL LIKE A FAILURE."	*COULD BE:*	"IF I GO BACK TO WORK AFTER CARING FOR MY SON FOR SO LONG, I'LL HAVE TO REFRESH MY SKILLS AND SPEND TIME LEARNING. BUT I'M WILLING TO PUT IN THE EFFORT."
"IF I TAKE UP EXERCISE, I'LL BE EMBARRASSED BECAUSE I'M SO OLD AND OUT OF SHAPE."	*COULD BE:*	"I'M READY TO EMBARK ON A NEW STAGE OF MY LIFE, AND I'M CAPABLE OF DEVELOPING A HIGHER LEVEL OF FITNESS EVEN IF IT'S HARD."

Like it or not, most of us suffer from some degree of spotlight effect. But stop to think about how often you consider the mistakes or choices others make that don't directly affect you. We're guessing you don't spend much mental energy on those, and neither do other people. Those around us aren't quick to label us a failure or a quitter. And they're likely to shift their mental picture of us if they witness our resilience. So the next time you find yourself shying away from something just because of a fear of failure, remember that such narratives are coming from you, not them. Other people are more patient, supportive, and forgiving of you than you might expect.

This is why practicing self-compassion is especially crucial during these early career years. Celebrate your own accomplishments, and remember that you alone are ultimately witness to your own life.

Try Before You Buy

In the Exploratory Stage, you have the advantage of a relatively blank slate. We encourage you to fearlessly embrace that freedom as you look ahead at your life. Regardless of how outlandish or unknown your career recommendations may seem, each one is worth careful thought. Treat these recommendations as invitations to explore. Read about, talk to, and shadow the professionals who work in jobs matched to your profile. A fuller understanding will help you to spot hidden or unexpected points of interest. Even for occupations you've never considered before, taking time to learn about the full range of activities involved can ultimately make you more certain of your final choice. Having lunch with your lawyer cousin to hear about his typical day could light a fire of motivation or, conversely, cause you to rethink spending three years and hundreds of thousands of dollars on law school. The earlier in your career you can seek out such discoveries, the better.

Maya Ziegler always wanted to work on a farm. When she begrudgingly attended college, she sought every opportunity to slip out of the classroom and into a barn. Her Specialist personality immediately drove her to seek out everything she could learn about the dairy industry, from the benefits of ryegrass to the shelf space on the grocery aisle. For Ziegler, this included hands-on experience on seven different farms, taking extra online courses on regenerative agriculture, and attending conferences and networking events. Her long shifts as a dairy apprentice, cleaning out stalls and milking cows, were driven by her reasoning: *Why not start at the source?*

By her midtwenties, however, Ziegler knew she needed more than an animal husbandry skill set; she needed a more complete picture of the food industry if she was going to make a meaningful impact. She was passionate about improving the viability of dairy farms in America, and she wanted to see some major changes in the way humans produce and consume food. To this end, Ziegler applied and gained employment with one of the largest producers of branded processed foods. Importantly, she chose a company with the purchasing muscle to accelerate sustainable agricultural practices. While this shift might sound counterintuitive, she recognized that a corporate background would give her the knowledge and power to make larger-scale change. "I knew I had a lot to learn," she told us, "and working for a large corporation that was investing in research and new approaches to agriculture would provide that." Broadening her lens from dairy to the larger food industry allowed her to identify opportunities within regenerative agriculture that she might never have otherwise considered. Ziegler likes to remind herself in moments of uncertainty that "at this stage I can—and should—play the long game."[7] Now, back on the farm, she is leveraging what she learned from her corporate experience to explore the innovative and disruptive ways of producing and marketing local dairy products.

Part of your ability to flex so much at this stage in life is due to the raw potential of aptitudes. The seeds of our skills, aptitudes lie dormant underground unless, or until, we are motivated to develop them through learning and practice. Even the strongest 3D Visualizers can't become architects overnight, and Concentrated Focusers must dedicate years of study and training before they become surgeons. In the Exploratory stage of life, building a portfolio of appropriate and transferable skills is crucially important, because the industries and roles you take on in ten years are likely to deviate from what you are doing now.

As you begin transitioning to the next stage in your life, whatever expertise you have mastered in your twenties becomes a kind of admission ticket to the next course, the learning and decision-making of our thirties and forties.

The Builders

If we only earned airline rewards points for every time we've heard a thirty-something say "I wish someone had told me this earlier!" we'd never have to pay for a flight again. But the truth is, it's never too late to retool your career and center your life around your authentic and natural talents. In the Building stage of your life, it is natural to look back on your twenties with wistful feelings. You may harbor regret or frustration about missed opportunities or things you wish you could redo, whether it's finishing a degree or learning more marketable skills. If you find yourself stalled at work, wondering if you've taken the wrong path, you are not alone. And even if you are confident in the choices you've made up to this point, it is important to realize that the portability of your skills is, in fact, more salient than whatever jobs you've held in the past.

Luckily, age blesses us with perspective, wisdom, and self-assurance. Knowing your unique talents and traits boosts these gains and makes it easier to recognize when it's time for a change. At this point in your life, even the smallest efforts can pay big dividends, helping you to find inspiration and reenergize. Your new awareness will help you make confident choices and pull off a smart, tactful shift rather than an abrupt or rash career switch.

When star softball player Stacie Townsend's neatly packaged plans exploded, she didn't just need to pivot, she had to do a complete one-eighty. It would be an understatement to say that she was disappointed to realize that her athletic career was sunsetting. She found she didn't know who she was or what she was capable of, because her identity had always been inseparable from softball. But Townsend is a rationalist through and through. She picked herself up and fixed her sights on a new career in law at the suggestion of a friend. She concentrated on a new goal with the same resolve she'd given softball; she didn't vacillate and she didn't look back. "I always felt like Elle Woods from the movie, *Legally Blonde*," says Townsend. "I guess I'll go to law school!"

And this would have been the end of Townsend's story, if not for a tugging that wouldn't go away. Accelerating fast at her law firm, Townsend still felt incomplete. Sports, the interest that had consumed much of her young life, was missing. Her parents were the first to notice their daughter was not altogether satisfied despite her obvious success. Early adopters of the now widely beloved game of Pickleball, Townsend's parents had a hunch this game could be their daughter's next thing. "Yes," says Townsend, "it was my parents who got me into Pickleball!" At first, it was simply "a new outlet, a way to get exercise." But it didn't take long for Townsend to get good. Really good. Soon she made it all the way to the US Open Pickleball Championships.

If you haven't been following the Pickleball hype the last few years, fueled by the likes of George Clooney and Ellen DeGeneres, it is a relatively simple game and easy to learn. A mix of tennis, badminton, and table tennis, Pickleball is the kind of sport you learn once and can play for a lifetime. Townsend told us the sport has become quite competitive as its popularity skyrockets. There are now millions of dollars in prize money out there and a major league. All of this was certainly exciting for Townsend, who thought her competitive sport career had ended long ago; she was reliving her glory days.

But a new phase of life reveals new goals, and Townsend realized that winning accolades, and even money, wasn't the only thing she was after. The sport became more than a competitive outlet when an unlikely business opportunity emerged from an even unlikelier problem: Townsend's mom wanted a new Pickleball shirt. She wasn't satisfied with the standard gear for women, which was usually generously adorned with, you guessed it, pickles. Townsend lit up with an idea, receiving that familiar jolt of excitement entrepreneurs get when they see an opportunity or untapped corner of the market. "That's when I decided I would start Pickler," says Townsend.

Today, Pickler is a content, media, merchandise, and resource site for Pickleball enthusiasts and newbies alike. "We're at 110,000 subscribers right now. I think last year we had 2 million visitors to the website," Townsend told us in the summer of 2023. But in true Builder fashion, Stacie Townsend is smart and calculated; she's not about to jump ship on her legal career, even if she is putting her all into this new side venture. She is a lawyer-entrepreneur, and she holds this hyphenated title proudly. She has found a way back to a life she loved in competitive sport, now with the help of her newly discovered enterprising spirit and problem-solving acumen. For Townsend, that has made all the difference.

People in the Building stage are also well positioned to close the exposure gap, or the void between the job opportunities that you think are out there and the openings that actually exist. At this point in our lives, we may have settled into marriage and family or lived through the pain of divorce; we have held several jobs; we are taking on the added responsibilities of caring for aging parents. For those who haven't yet decided whether to go to graduate school or have kids, they almost certainly will choose by the time they're fifty.

By this stage, we have also learned important practical lessons about saving and spending, paying our monthly bills, and navigating taxes, tuition, health, and life insurance. We've weathered losses and wins, ego boosts and crushing disappointments. Of course, we're still learning, but with the perspective gleaned of age, we are now better equipped to make informed decisions about what we do and don't like. In contrast to the Exploratory stage, in the Building stage our interests have grown more influenced by our previous exposure and experience, which means we can trust them a bit more.

Is This a Mistake?: Facing the Midlife Career Switch

Stephenie Riley (the engineer-turned-naturopathic doctor) chose to change course midway through her career. Determined to reenergize her life, she heroically faced the "sunk cost bias"—the common illusion that leaving an established career comes with costs due to previous investments of time and money—and started anew.

There were many obstacles, including the well-meaning criticism and doubt from loved ones. At the time, the discipline of naturopathy was new, so she had no guarantee that the money and years she invested in a degree would pay off. But as a woman in her thirties, she had enough work experience and exposure to know what would truly hold her interest. When she later received the results of her YouScience assessment, Riley discovered that "Naturopath" was one of her top career recommendations (along with "Engineering"; there are many different jobs that can fit any given aptitude profile!). As she describes it, the decision to shift careers surprised even her. It was "clearly a huge leap," she says, and "super atypical for my personality and my life path." But she drew inspiration from the story of a friend's father who had gone back to school to become a dentist in his thirties. Hearing that helped Riley believe switching careers might be possible; it "kind of opened up the doors" and made her realize "it's not entirely insane," even if that's what many of the people around her were saying.[8]

Riley didn't just make a midlife career change. Like so many Americans, she invested time and money in additional education to pursue this goal. In the United States today, the average age for graduate school students is thirty-three, and 22 percent of graduates are over forty years old (8 percent are over the age of fifty). With the accumulated wisdom of their age, these midlife dreamers are well equipped to confidently focus their priorities and pursue their true calling.

Finding a Post-Combat Career

The day Zach Leggett, the Green Beret who became an ICEE executive, signed out of the army, he felt simultaneously exhilarated and overwhelmed. He was thrilled by the possibility of taking on a radically new line of work. But what, exactly, would that be? His assessment results revealed a wide range of ways Leggett could apply his talents beyond the military, and he initially felt unsettled. For the first time in his adult life, he wasn't obligated to follow orders. But it also felt like a huge departure. Over the course of twenty-two years, he had grown comfortable as a military leader, and "in civilian life I thought I would be starting all over," he recalls. Still, he vowed to keep an open mind. "At first I didn't see the parallels between my work in the military and running operations at a frozen carbonated beverage company," he laughs, "but I told myself I'd never say 'no' to an introduction." Staying true to his talents, he reinvented his career by drawing on his existing experience and applying it to a new domain. The transition was surprisingly seamless.

Every year, approximately 200,000 men and women like Leggett leave the US military and transition to civilian life. The US Department of Labor's Transition Assistance Program helps veterans find career opportunities in corporate America, where they find surprising new ways to repurpose their skills. For example, the program educates Special Forces veterans on how they can adapt to roles in private security, intelligence analysis, medicine, and more.

Leggett supports this work by guiding other vets who are making the transition to civilian life, mentoring them with empathy and understanding. "These tremendous individuals have a lot more to give," says Leggett. "And they can continue to be exceptional in whatever they want to do."[9] Leggett also likes to remind his mentees that fulfillment in life comes from many other things beyond our jobs.

The Pros

Once we pass fifty, changes in technology, organizational structures, and society as a whole may contribute to feelings of obsolescence. You find yourself asking: *How many times will I need to learn how to use a new customer relationship management tool?* Or *Do I really report to a twenty-seven-year-old?* Or *Do my years of experience mean nothing at this firm anymore?* In these darker moments, it's important to remember that the pressure to retool and re-skill doesn't just weigh heavy on those nearing retirement. It is a feature of the digital era, a requirement for everyone regardless of age.

In the Pro stage, the trick is to recognize which of your talents or strengths you can most easily repurpose and seek out opportunities to share those skills with others. In the process, your unique experience and expertise will evolve and retain its relevance.[10]

Consider Carla Hall, the celebrity chef and unstoppable entrepreneur. Now in her fifties, Hall seems to be accelerating rather than slowing down. She's hosting television shows, authoring children's books, and judging national gingerbread contests. She's even working on inventing some of her own products. Inspired by the common challenge of the wilting herbs that litter so many refrigerator drawers, she told us about her "idea for an herb keeper . . . one that fits right in your refrigerator door." While Hall's fame makes her a person in high demand, her experience helps her to recognize which requests to pursue and which to politely decline. She is careful to engage only in activities that will energize, rather than deplete, her abilities. As she told us, "I'm a borderline introvert-extrovert. I find it easy to talk to people. But I have to come back and recharge in a creative space of my own, which is why I'm doing art."[11]

What If the Career I Love Abandons Me?

Technology has wrought dramatic changes in almost every industry, altering not just the nature of work and workplaces but the daily lives of workers. Tal Howell was first drawn to her career in graphic design in the years when X-Acto knives and glue sticks were requisite; and little thought was given to the digital tools that might one day arrive. She immediately felt a resonance between graphic design and her strongest aptitudes (as a 3D Visualizer and Brainstormer), and the work also satisfied her amplifying capabilities (discriminating between shades of colors and manual dexterity). In particular, she loved the physical nature of cutting out the pieces and parts for each design, then creating the layout and marking it up with color and instructions for the engraver.

A lifelong learner, Howell was quick to adopt new tools such as In-Design, Sketch, and Adobe Illustrator as they became available. But she soon felt an acute sense of loss, as her creative process morphed from manipulating physical materials to navigating a screen using a mouse. While she still enjoyed formulating designs—coming up with a concept, selecting the proper colors and hues, and choosing fonts—she craved an outlet for the aptitudes no longer used at her job. Rather than abandon her livelihood, she began sewing soft furnishings and delving into inventive upholstery as an extension of her design studio.

If you are over fifty, your results are most likely to articulate and reinforce the skills you already knew you had. For Joel Savitt (director of Google Developer Studio), it felt like opening his eyes to see something he already felt was there. Speaking of how he discovered he was a Diagnostic Problem Solver, he commented: "I hadn't considered how, for most of my career, I've been in position after position which required me to make big decisions with only scant information in front of me." For example, "even 20 years ago as the Coordinating Producer of 'The Amazing Race' in Season 2, I was chasing contestants around the world with camera crews and only scant information and communication tools to work with. Locating the contestants always presented a challenge. I was making my best guess at where they might turn up. And our primary modes of communication back then were satellite phones as there was no GPS! I see how dealing with ambiguity has always been a power alley for me."[12]

The Pro stage of life is full of great gains and important decisions. You can maximize new opportunities by knowing how to frame and mobilize your accumulated experiences and areas of expertise around your unique and time-tested natural gifts. By nurturing a growth mindset, you can launch into this third phase of your career with an agenda all your own. People over fifty have earned seniority in their careers, resulting in greater flexibility and autonomy. If you're a parent whose children have recently flown the nest, you may be lucky enough to have ample free time and choose to go back to work, step up your career involvement, or even pursue the training or education you've been eyeing for years. This is likely the time when you can lean into greater risk-taking and engagement in work and volunteer opportunities.

If you are contemplating retirement from paid work, your assessment results can also help you decide what to do next. For Betsy, her uncle Bill Mathis has been an inspiration in this regard. For over thirty years, Bill worked as a trader in the municipal bond department at Morgan Keegan, a large investment banking and wealth management firm headquartered in Memphis, Tennessee. A Diagnostic Problem Solver, he loved making fast decisions under pressure. But following a company merger in 2012, he chose to retire early. With his children grown and some money put away, he sought new outlets for his talents. Soon he was training as a volunteer in an emergency medical response unit. He now spends three nights a week accompanying medical and law enforcement teams as they answer emergency calls—the perfect outlet for his Diagnostic Problem-Solving skills.

Even at this later stage of your life, you can leave your job or start afresh—but your hidden genius never leaves you. When Alex was growing up, her mother, Jeanne Whited, always worked the night shift at a local restaurant. She'd don her white shirt, black pants, and well-worn Dansko clogs and head out to wait tables as soon as Alex's dad got home from his job as a traveling wine distributor. Over the years, the restaurants where her mom worked changed hands, but she continued to serve others.

Still, she always dreamed of running her own restaurant. While she was raising a family, however, the risks—and the necessary commitment of time and money—were too daunting. Finally, at age sixty-two, she and Alex's father stumbled upon an old building that had been previously occupied by a greasy-spoon diner. It was located in a remote drive-through town in Northern California, the perfect place for retirement. Instead, Jeanne saw it and thought, *This is it! This will be my restaurant!* With more time, fewer family responsibilities, and a higher tolerance for risk, she created a bustling new eatery that people now drive hours to enjoy. And when Jeanne later saw the results of her YouScience assessment, no one was surprised to find that *head chef* was one of her top career suggestions—a near-perfect match.

What If My Job Doesn't Tick All the Boxes?

Regardless of the stage of life we are in or how much we know about ourselves, very few of us will hold a single job that manages to satisfy all our most prominent aptitudes, personality traits, and interests for decades. In other words, hitting periodic speedbumps, where you feel adrift or stuck in your job, is completely normal—in fact, it is to be expected. At such times it is tempting to put our jobs on the witness stand as we search for the root of our dissatisfaction. But job dissatisfaction is actually an indicator that one or more of our core aptitudes is stagnating. In reality, we've probably just started drifting away from our strongest abilities, and it's time for a course correction.

When dissatisfaction or boredom starts setting in, we recommend seeking out informal leisure activities, interests, volunteer work, and other avocations that not only fulfill you but make use of your aptitudes. Even more than our jobs, these varied pursuits are crucial to feeling happy and fulfilled. Chris Karlsmose, a consultant for the management firm Bain & Company, makes intentional use of his downtime by playing the miniature war game Warhammer 40,000. It's "a great outlet from work," he noted.[13] But it has also tapped into something much deeper. Now a Warhammer World Champion, Karlsmose battles with friends in a world of legendary heroes, gruesome beasts, and

flying monsters, indulging his aptitudes for brainstorming and strategic thinking.

Like Karlsmose, finding ways to flex your aptitudes outside of your
paid work can help you strike a balance. We often dismiss leisure activities as relatively insignificant because they don't bring us any material
benefit. Yet our hobbies can play a key role not only in unlocking happiness and fulfillment, but helping us avoid burnout.

If you find yourself asking *Why am I bored?* or *Why am I so tired at
the end of the day?* the answers to these questions can help you look
past the more obvious material or emotional reasons to uncover what's
really going on. For example, a thought such as *I hate my job and need
to quit* might shift to *My boss is ineffective, and I need to move somewhere else within this company.* Approaching our dissatisfaction from
this perspective helps us to find less drastic, life-altering solutions than
simply quitting. And if you discover that your job really *is* the problem,
framing your discontent in terms of your underutilized aptitudes can
help you find ways to improve things by switching your role or handing
off certain tasks to someone else.

The knowledge, confidence, and direction we gain from recognition
of our talents help us to identify more specific causes and proactively
explore solutions, rather than target our jobs, in general. And not quitting allows us to pivot without having to find a new job or face financial insecurity. As the psychologist and academic Angela Duckworth
suggests, you should never leave your job on a bad day or give up on
something when you are experiencing "acute disappointment."[14]

It might also be that the job that used to get you out of bed in the
morning has lost its luster. Maybe you've gradually become jaded or
disillusioned. Whatever the cause, reconnecting with your innate gifts
can help you refocus. For example, when Chicago-area teacher Tracy
Crowley began feeling less satisfied with her job, she decided to experiment with a new work-life balance. In college, Crowley had stepped off

the pre-law track and made a beeline for a career in education, where she had been truly happy and fulfilled for many years. Her superiors noted her dedication and enthusiasm and set her on the fast track to leadership. "I was on every committee, and very soon I was in a teacher-leadership role," she remembers. She also started earning a handsome salary.

But about fifteen years in, Crowley started seeing changes. "I felt like my hands were tied by the new policies in our district," she told us. "I wasn't able to do what I wanted to do in classrooms and schools as an instructional coach, and it felt like the system was really crushing innovative teachers." Still, she cares deeply about education. And with less than a decade left before she retires with her full pension, quitting her job just didn't make sense.

So, in her forties, Crowley started looking for opportunities outside the classroom that might invigorate both her and her school. Since then, she's earned National Geographic Society's prestigious Grosvenor Teacher Fellowship, which sent her to Antarctica with a team of researchers. As a curriculum writer, she's contributed to the Pulitzer Center on Crisis Reporting. She even manages a global nonprofit. And in the free time afforded by her academic schedule, she pursues unique side projects that tap into her talents and passions. "I am no longer simply developing a rich career," says Crowley. "At this stage, I am developing a rich life."[15]

Like Crowley, you may garner a paycheck that allows you to find happiness outside of work. Or maybe you're retired and are hoping to find a level of fulfillment you never found at your job. You could still be seeking paid work that can contribute to your life and your financial security. Whatever your situation, knowing what you're getting yourself into (or out of, as the case may be) will help you determine whether you need to step away from either finding your dream job, or what you once thought was that job. And knowing your hidden genius will allow you to make these decisions with confidence. Like an electric current, it feeds your satisfaction and fulfillment throughout your life. All you have to do is stay plugged in.

The Power of Self-Awareness

Well done! Having explored your aptitudes, interests, and personal approach, you are now an expert in you. With this knowledge in hand, you are fully equipped to make informed decisions and claim greater agency in all aspects of your career.

Now it's time to grab hold of what you have learned and use it to steer your life.

Your YouScience results offer you a tangible map to guide your future, along with the words to explain and share it with others. Nellie Davis, a member of the Walker River Paiute Tribe in Nevada, says that, in her tradition, young people are asked not "What do you want to be when you grow up?" but "What will be your medicine to the world?" Viewed from this perspective, our work in the world has healing power and our talents are not just ours to covet; they are meant to be shared. As Davis explained, these individual gifts can heal and improve the lives of those around us.[16]

We invite you to joyfully meet the challenge. Honor your hidden genius.

Appendix

Aptitudes for Pay and Pleasure

The following (incomplete) list offers some examples of the types of work and leisure activities that benefit from specific aptitudes. Just because an activity is or isn't on this list doesn't mean that a person with the associated aptitude should or shouldn't do it, or wouldn't love it. But in general, each of the following careers and physical, intellectual, or creative pastimes includes key elements that can help satisfy specific aptitudes and bring you fulfillment. They are listed alphabetically and grouped under their corresponding aptitudes.

3D VISUALIZER

A Genuine Plus for the Professional: Aerospace engineer; Architect; Athletic coach; Carpenter; Chef; Computer programmer; Dentist; Firefighter; Graphic designer; Hairstylist; Interior designer; Mechanical engineer; Physical therapist; Scientist; Tidewater architect; Urban planner; Videographer.

Why Not Try: Ballroom dance; Billiards or pool; Choreography; Geocaching; Golf; Hip-hop dance; Jigsaw puzzles; LEGO; Martial arts; Origami; Photography or filmmaking; Quilting or sewing; Riflery; Sailing; Sculpting; Woodworking.

ABSTRACT THINKER

A Genuine Plus for the Professional: Clergy; Consultant; Counselor; Financial adviser; Fundraiser; Hiring manager; Human resources professional; Lawyer; Lobbyist; Paralegal; Psychotherapist; Researcher; Salesperson (services); Social worker; Speech pathologist; Teacher; University administrator.

Why Not Try: Academic lectures; Blogging; Book clubs; Bridge; Comparative literature; Conversation games (e.g., Cards Against Humanity, Film Festivals, Genealogy, Malarkey, Table Topics); Cycling; Hiking; Kayaking; Meditation; Mentoring; Paddleboarding; Philosophy; Podcasting; Poker; Running; Singing or songwriting; Swimming; Tutoring.

SPACE PLANNER

A Genuine Plus for the Professional: Arts administrator; Book editor; Construction manager; Data analyst; Event planner; Groundskeeper; Logistics manager; Nurse; Office manager; Property manager; Real estate developer; Retail manager; Sales (products); Security specialist; Technical writer.

Why Not Try: Antiquing; Bird-watching; Brewing; Camping; Car shows; Cooking; Crossword puzzles; Debate; Fishing; Flower arranging; Furniture restoration; Geocaching; Metal-detecting; Mixology; Model kits; Pickleball; Tennis; Yoga.

BRAINSTORMER

A Genuine Plus for the Professional: Actor, Advertising specialist; Coach; Consultant; Corporate trainer; Designer; Entrepreneur; Event planner; Fundraiser; Graphic designer; Journalist; Litigator; Marketer; Public relations manager; Sales; Social media influencer; Songwriter; Sports agent; Teacher; Videographer.

Why Not Try: Acting; Blogging; Choreography; Composing; Content creation; Cooking; Creative writing; Debate clubs and tournaments; Improvisational comedy; Jewelry making; Music therapy; Painting; Party games (e.g., Charades, Cranium, or Pictionary); Photography; Poetry or slam poetry; Public speaking; Songwriting; Storytelling; Volunteer fundraising.

CONCENTRATED FOCUSER

A Genuine Plus for the Professional: Accountant; Aesthetician; Anesthesiologist; Auditor; Auto mechanic; Bookkeeper; Coder; Compliance officer; Curator; Dental hygienist; Engineer; Executive assistant; Insurance salesperson; Loan officer; Medical technician; Nurse; Occupational therapist; Pharmacist; Physical therapist; Pilot; Programmer; Risk officer; Script editor; Social worker; Video editor.

Why Not Try: Aikido; Archery; Ballet; Bonsai; Bread making; Bridge; Calligraphy; Dressage; Glass blowing; Golf; Marksmanship; Martial arts; Meditation; Musical composition; Practicing musical instruments; Rock climbing; Rowing; Running; Scuba; Swimming; Video games; Yoga.

IDEA CONTRIBUTOR

A Genuine Plus for the Professional: Architectural draftsman; Attorney; Blockchain engineer; Counselor; Data scientist; Dentist; Editor;

Electrical engineer; Facilitator; Financial adviser; Financial analyst; Ghostwriter; Grant writer; Hiring manager; Human resource specialist; Logistician; Mediator; Meeting or convention planner; Radiologist; Researcher; School administrator; Statistician; Veterinarian.

Why Not Try: Brewing; Facilitation; Fundraising; Mentoring; Photography; Scrapbooking; Snorkeling; Tutoring; Video gaming; Volunteer leadership.

DIAGNOSTIC PROBLEM SOLVER

A Genuine Plus for the Professional: Appraiser; Archaeologist; Arts, music, or entertainment critic; Athletic coach; Attorney; Design engineer; Diagnostician; Editor; EMT; Event planner; Game designer; Journalist; Judge; Naturopath; Plumber; Police officer; Politician; Private investigator; Referee; Trader; Veterinarian; Writer.

Why Not Try: Basketball; Comparative literature; Crisis hotline volunteer; Emergency response team volunteer; Escape games; Game shows; Judging (e.g., at dog, flower, or horse shows, ice-skating competitions, et cetera); Mystery novels or shows; Party games (e.g., Charades); Pickleball; Ping-Pong; Soccer; Tennis; Volleyball.

FACT CHECKER

A Genuine Plus for the Professional: Accountant; Bookkeeper; Chemist; Compliance officer; Financial analyst; Help desk technician; Hiring manager; Historian; Investigative journalist; Loan officer; Opposition researcher; Pediatrician; Pharmacist; Professor; Quality assurance officer; Risk officer.

Why Not Try: Baking; Bird-watching; Gardening; Identifying and cataloging wildflowers; Piloting; Poll worker; Quilting; Scuba diving; Sewing; Stamp collecting; Woodworking.

INVESTIGATOR

A Genuine Plus for the Professional: Airfield operations specialist; Bank teller; Blockchain engineer; Dog trainer; Engineer; Horticulturist; Human resources manager; Insurance actuary; Physician's assistant; Project manager; Sound technician; Teacher.

Why Not Try: Chaperoning school events; Making home movies; Murder mystery dinners; Timing or judging races or competitions; Volunteer training guide dogs.

SEQUENTIAL THINKER

A Genuine Plus for the Professional: Accountant; Actuary; Athletic trainer; Bioinformatics specialist; Campaign manager; Consultant; Contractor; Corporate strategist; Digital forensics analyst; Economist; Editor; Electrician; Engineer; Event planner; Financial planner; Lawyer; Office manager; Physician; Professional organizer; Real estate developer; Scientist; Social media manager; Software developer; Stylist; Teacher; Tidewater architect; Tour guide; Travel agent; Wedding planner; Writer.

Why Not Try: Cooking for large groups; Organizing photo albums and memory books; Planning dinners and events; Planning vacations; Putting on the school play.

PROCESS SUPPORTER

A Genuine Plus for the Professional: Banker; Building inspector; Chief financial officer; Compliance officer; Corporate controller; Cybersecurity expert; Document manager; Health inspector; Human resource specialist; Inventory management specialist; Medical transcriptionist; Paralegal; Risk officer; Tax assessor.

Why Not Try: Baking; Helping at a library; Judging flower shows;

Refereeing sports games; Serving as a board treasurer; Serving as a state delegate; Teaching ballet; Volunteering as a parliamentarian.

COLLABORATIVE PLANNER

A Genuine Plus for the Professional: Art director; Blockchain engineer; Clergy; Curriculum developer; Information security engineer; Insurance claims examiner; Logistics manager; Management analyst; Occupational therapist; Production line supervisor; Real estate agent; Social worker; Training and development specialist.

Why Not Try: Bowling; Coaching youth sports; Football; Ice hockey; Public service; Rowing; Soccer; Teaching youth religious studies; Training a service dog; Volunteering on a nonprofit board.

Acknowledgments

We were in different places, in different stages, and in different careers when we began this project. It was just before the global Covid pandemic in 2020. Betsy was preparing her TEDx talk on aptitudes, a subject she'd been passionate about for decades. Having cofounded an online career platform aimed at young adults in 2011, she had already seen countless lives transformed with the confirmation and knowledge provided by aptitude assessments. She was motivated to write a book because she understood from personal experience that all individuals, no matter what life stage they were in, could benefit.

Twenty years her junior, Alex had a young child at home and was building a private counseling practice, which incorporated YouScience as a foundational tool to guide her clients. She encountered and helped many who were trapped in living up to others' definitions of success, or worse, assuming they didn't have any noteworthy talents at all. She knew more people than her small caseload of clients needed to be made aware of their innate gifts.

Our shared conviction that many of us are unaware of our potential emboldened us to write this book. With each interview we conducted, it became increasingly obvious that we weren't just writing a book; we were on an urgent mission. We drew energy and encouragement from the heartwarming and funny stories we heard from individuals who had gained newfound and transformative knowledge of their aptitudes through the assessment.

But there would be no great aha's or changed lives without the dogged determination of a small group of people who were integral to democratizing an assessment of aptitudes that was previously only available to those with the means to travel to an in-person evaluation center. First thanks goes to Betsy's YouScience cofounder, Richard Patton, a person of vision and courage, who marshaled every resource at his disposal to launch a transformative company. Equal appreciation is given for the extraordinary contribution and support of Anna Ball and the entire Ball Foundation, who invested and shared their aptitude research, as well as Philip Hardin, the mission-driven CEO of YouScience.

A scientific assessment like this is informed by years of psychometric testing and research. Dr. Rich Feller, a celebrated academic and one of the most respected leaders in the field of self-awareness, career fit, and intentional career development, advised and made key introductions for us. In particular, he led us to individuals at HumRRO, especially Rod McCloy, who has been so generous with his time and scholarship. We're grateful for their enthusiasm, encouragement, and thoughtful insights throughout.

In addition, there would be no packaged book if not for the brilliant women, who are essentially alchemists, who helped us sculpt messy, complex, and nuanced information into lines on a page. We thank our literary agent, Eve MacSweeney, for believing in the importance of our idea and for guiding us to ensure that it became a reality. Lauren Lipton whipped us into shape when we needed it most, telling us to "stay hydrated" and just get it done when we were crafting our first proposal. We're grateful for her expert advice during the development stage. Bronwyn Fryer contributed immensely from outline to final copy, and we could not have accomplished any of this without her humor, patience, and wit. We must also thank Bronwyn's stalwart colleague, Emily Donaldson, for her research assistance and attention to the finer points of citations and endnotes. Critically, we thank our editor at Harvest, Sarah Pelz, who has the rare gift of renewing an author's excitement and energy for their work. She not only believed in us; she quite possibly believed in us more than we believed in ourselves.

Finally, we are forever indebted to the countless people who agreed to sit with us for an interview, long before the book had a publisher. These early believers trusted us enough to share their time and stories. Though not all of our interviews made it into the final manuscript, each and every one guided, taught, and challenged us, helping us craft the book you're reading today. There would be no book without their honest and raw reflections.

Betsy

It all began from the advice of my best friend since grade school, Susan Simons. We've been through nearly every life stage together, and it was she who suggested to me during one of my career crises that I visit Johnson O'Connor to have my aptitudes assessed. I'm forever grateful. Thank you also to my cute friend Patti Smallwood who was game enough to join me on that fateful road trip to Atlanta. We've had fun laughing about it ever since. As I mentioned before, the company You-Science, from which this all derives, would not have happened had I not been working with the visionary Richard Patton. His energy, optimism, and ability to attract so many others to the concept were essential. I am grateful to so many other passionate believers, including Ed Powell, a brilliant data scientist, Laura Cooper, a wordsmith beyond measure, and Mark Reiter, a supportive adviser and friend. It is undeniable that "Jesus had the wheel" when he put the extraordinary Donna and

David Campbell in my path as it was they who made the crucial introduction to my spectacular agent, Eve.

So many others sustained me in the process. Thank you to Susan Basham, Victor Boschini, Cathy Brown, Mark Cannon, Andy Chan, Teresa Chope, John Cooper, Nicole Driver, Frank Drummond, Marshall Goldsmith, Cathy Grier, Greg Hagood, Mimi Howe, Emily James, Sue Joyce, Cyril Le Lay, Rod Lowman, Ann Marie and Martin McNamara, Keith Meacham, Vanessa Morse, Reed Nirula, Victoria Pao, Elizabeth Papel, Jennifer Puryear, Yvonne Ralsky, Alice Randall, Trish Ring, Jim Shelton, Jeremy Snow, Bill Spitz, Heidi Stamer, Adam Taggart, Margaret Tezak, Suzy Welch, Grayson Wills, Meade Wills, Ridley Wills IV, and my mah-jongg and bridge group.

Most important, I am overwhelmingly grateful to my loyal and patient husband, Ridley.

Alex

My interest in career navigation and the job-hopping phenomenon began while working in rural Nevada, helping kids get an early look at vocational choice before graduating high school. I knew very little about work-based learning and career education at that point, and I am grateful to Michelle Lewis and Miya Mackenzie for trusting me with this work when I was a novice. Thanks to the Embassy of Switzerland in Washington, DC, for giving me a ThinkSwiss research grant to get to the source of the "schnupperlehre" (a sort of sneak peek internship in Switzerland). This pivotal experience set me on the course that led me to this book. In my ongoing learning about career choice, I thank Dr. Katherine Caves, Dr. Hans-Ulrich Grunder, Dr. Sarah Schilliger, Dr. Peter Streckeisen, Bob Potts, and Karsten Heise for freely sharing their wisdom and research.

Thank you to the colleagues, friends, and longtime supporters of my work, including David Geddes, Matt McIver, Caroline and Kurosh Moassessi, Kendra and Donny Newsome, Adam Robinson, Andrea Ross, Rick and Corine Winfield, and Peggy Wynne Borgman.

Finally, to my family for their enthusiasm for every success and quick dismissal of every failure. Especially to my husband, Jonas, and daughter, Rory, for ensuring I never take my work—or myself—too seriously, reminding me what matters most, and buckling up beside me for what's been an incredible ride.

Notes

All ages, titles, employment statuses, and other details pertaining to interviewees in this book were recorded at the time of the interview.

INTRODUCTION

1. Alan Gribben, "Mark Twain, Phrenology and the 'Temperaments': A Study of Pseudoscientific Influence," *American Quarterly* 24, no. 1 (1972): 45–68; and Madeleine B. Stern, "Mark Twain Had His Head Examined," *American Literature* 41, no. 2 (1969): 207–218.

2. Mark Twain, *The Autobiography of Mark Twain*, ed. Charles Neider (New York: Harper & Brothers, 1959), 65.

3. Ashley Stahl, "The Last of the Great Resignation?" *Forbes*, June 9, 2022, https://www.forbes.com/sites/ashleystahl/2022/06/09/the-last-of-the-great-resignation.

4. "State of the Global Workplace: 2022 Report," Gallup, https://www.gallup.com/workplace/349484/state-of-the-global-workplace.aspx.

5. Ryan A. Decker and John Haltiwanger, "Business entry and exit in the Covid-19 pandemic: A preliminary look at official data," Board of Governors of the Federal Reserve System, May 6, 2022, https://www.federalreserve.gov/econres/notes/feds-notes/business-entry-and-exit-in-the-covid-19-pandemic-a-preliminary-look-at-official-data-20220506.html.

6. Elise Gould and Jori Kandra, "Wages grew in 2020 because the bottom fell out of the low-wage labor market: The State of Working America in 2020 Wages Report," Economic Policy Institute, February 14, 2021, https://www.epi.org/publication/state-of-working-america-wages-in-2020.

7. Hailey Mensik, "Healthcare lost 30K jobs in January," *Healthcare Dive*, February 5, 2021, https://www.healthcaredive.com/news/healthcare-lost-30K-jobs-in-January-BLS/594635.

8. Misty L. Heggeness, Jason Fields, Yazmin A. Garcia Trejo, and Anthony Schulzetenberg, "Tracking Job Losses for Mothers of School-Age Children During a Health Crisis," US Census Bureau, March 3, 2021, https://www.census.gov/library/stories

/2021/03/moms-work-and-the-pandemic.html; and Rashida Kamal, "Quitting is just half the story: the truth behind the 'Great Resignation,'" *Guardian*, January 4, 2022, https://www.theguardian.com/business/2022/jan/04/great-resignation-quitting -us-unemployment-economy.

9. Kim Parker, Juliana Menasce Horowitz, and Rachel Minkin, "How the Coronavirus has—and hasn't—changed the way Americans work," Pew Research Center, December 9, 2020, https://www.pewresearch.org/social-trends/2020/12/09/how-the -coronavirus-outbreak-has-and-hasnt-changed-the-way-americans-work.

10. Nikita Ovtchinikov, personal communication, September 13, 2022. All quotes from personal communications are included with the speaker's permission.

11. Corinne Reichert, "Over 80% of workers don't want to go back to the office full time, survey finds," *CNET*, March 25, 2021, https://www.cnet.com/health/over-80 -of-workers-dont-want-to-go-back-to-the-office-full-time-survey-finds; and Jessica Dickler, "'Great Resignation' gains steam as return-to-work plans take effect," CNBC, June 29, 2021, https://www.cnbc.com/2021/06/29/more-people-plan-to-quit-as -return-to-work-plans-go-into-effect-.html.

12. "Number of Jobs, Labor Market Experience, Marital Status, and Health: Results from a National Longitudinal Survey," US Bureau of Labor Statistics, August 31, 2021, https://www.bls.gov/news.release/pdf/nlsoy.pdf; Lauren Medina, Shannon Sabo, and Jonathan Vespa, "Living Longer: Historical and Projected Life Expectancy in the United States, 1960 to 2060," US Census Bureau, February 2020, p. 3, https://www.census.gov/content/dam/Census/library/publications/2020/demo /p25-1145.pdf; and Kenneth Terrell, "Who's Working More? People Age 65 and Older," AARP, November 22, 2019, https://www.aarp.org/work/careers/surging-older -workforce.

13. Lindsay Ellis and Angela Yang, "If Your Co-Workers Are 'Quiet Quitting,' Here's What That Means," *Wall Street Journal*, August 12, 2022, https://www.wsj.com /articles/if-your-gen-z-co-workers-are-quiet-quitting-heres-what-that-means -11660260608.

14. On average Americans today shift jobs frequently, and 30 percent change jobs every twelve months. While we generally hold between five and seven careers in our working lives, the average total number of jobs we will have had by the time we retire is twelve. "Number of Jobs, Labor Market Experience, Marital Status, and Health: Results from a National Longitudinal Survey," Bureau of Labor Statistics, August 2021, https://www.bls.gov/news.release/pdf/nlsoy.pdf.

15. Jessica Schieder and Elise Gould, "'Women's work' and the gender pay gap," Economic Policy Institute, July 20, 2016, https://www.epi.org/publication /womens-work-and-the-gender-pay-gap-how-discrimination-societal-norms -and-other-forces-affect-womens-occupational-choices-and-their-pay; Kevin A. Hoff, Kenneth E. Granillo-Velasquez, Alexis Hanna, Mike Morris, Hannah S. Nelson, and Frederick L. Oswald, "Interested and employed? A national study of gender differences in basic interests and employment," *Journal of Vocational Behavior* 148

(2024): 103942, https://doi.org/10.1016/j.jvb.2023.103942; and Rodney A. McCloy, Patrick J. Rottinghaus, Chan Jeong Park, Rich Feller, and Todd Bloom, "YouScience: Mitigating the skills gap by addressing the gender imbalance in high-demand careers," *Industrial and Organizational Psychology* 13, no. 3 (2020): 426–441.

16. John Oliver Siy, Adriana Germano, Laura Vianna, Jovani Azpeitia, Shaoxiong Yan, Amanda K. Montoya, and Sapna Cheryan, "Does the follow-your-passions ideology cause greater academic and occupational gender disparities than other cultural ideologies?" *Journal of Personality and Social Psychology* 125, no. 3 (2023), https://doi .org/10.1037/pspi0000421.

17. R. D. Laing, *Self and Others*, vol. 2 (London: Routledge, 1999).

18. J. P. Mortenson, "What Makes the Perfect Swimmer's Body?" *Swimming World*, March 5, 2023, https://www.swimmingworldmagazine.com/news/what-makes-the -perfect-swimmers-body.

19. Rebecca, personal communication, March 25, 2015.

20. Daphne Martschenko, "The IQ test wars: why screening for intelligence is still so controversial," *Conversation*, October 10, 2017, https://theconversation.com/the-iq -test-wars-why-screening-for-intelligence-is-still-so-controversial-81428.

21. Rodney A. McCloy, Patrick J. Rottinghaus, Chan Jeong Park, Rich Feller, and Todd Bloom, "YouScience: Mitigating the skills gap by addressing the gender imbalance in high-demand careers," *Industrial and Organizational Psychology* 13, no. 3 (2020): 426–441; and Alyson Klein, "Aptitude Tests: Are They Effective in Opening Students' Minds to More Career Paths?" *Education Week*, April 27, 2021, https://www .edweek.org/technology/aptitude-tests-are-they-effective-in-opening-students -minds-to-more-career-paths/2021/04.

22. Rodney A. McCloy and Betsy M. Wills, "STEM Careers and the Fourth Industrial Revolution: Filling the Skills Gap," *Career Planning & Adult Development Network Journal* 37, no. 2 (2021): 68–83.

23. Adam Grant, "The Perils of Following Your Career Passion," TED Talk, March 27, 2019, https://www.ted.com/talks/worklife_with_adam_grant_the_perils_of_following _your_career_passion.

24. Aidan F. Ryan, "Harvard Law School Increasingly Favors Applicants with Real-World Work Experience," *Harvard Crimson*, September 13, 2018, https://www .thecrimson.com/article/2018/9/13/law-school-work-experience.

25. Kim Severson, "'Top Chef' Dreams Crushed by Student Loan Debt," *New York Times*, May 8, 2007, https://www.nytimes.com/2007/05/08/us/08default.html.

26. College Data Analytics Team, "2023 Criminal Justice & Corrections Degree Guide," College Factual, https://www.collegefactual.com/majors/protective-security -safety-services/criminal-justice-and-corrections; and "Detectives and Criminal Investigators," *O*NET OnLine*, https://www.onetonline.org/link/summary/33-3021.00 ?redir=33-3021.01.

27. Kendra Cherry, "What Are the Big 5 Personality Traits?" *Verywell Mind*, March 11, 2023, https://www.verywellmind.com/the-big-five-personality-dimensions-2795422.

CHAPTER 1: WELCOME TO
YOUR HIDDEN GENIUS

1. Simone Giertz, personal communication, August 15, 2022.
2. Simone Giertz, "I Turned My Tesla into a Pickup Truck," YouTube, June 18, 2019, https://www.youtube.com/watch?v=jKv_N0IDS2A&t=2s.
3. Nicholas Lore, *The Pathfinder: How to Choose or Change Your Career for a Lifetime of Satisfaction and Success* (New York: Touchstone Books, 2011), 220.
4. Overton Thompson, personal communication, July 11, 2021.
5. William T. Sherman, *William T. Sherman Papers: General Correspondence, 1837–1891; 1855, July 12–1856, July 2*, image 280, Library of Congress, https://www.loc.gov/resource/mss39800.003_0346_0656.
6. Lysander Salmon Richards, *Vocophy: The New Profession* (Marlboro, MA: Pratt Brothers, Steam Job Printers, 1881), 102–3.
7. Richards, *Vocophy*, 87–100.
8. Frank Parsons, *Choosing a Vocation* (Boston: Houghton Mifflin, 1909), 5.
9. Johnson O'Connor, "Taking a Man's Measure: A Practical Study of Aptitudes," *Atlantic*, June 1931, https://www.theatlantic.com/magazine/archive/1931/06/taking-a-mans-measure-a-practical-study-of-aptitudes/650579.
10. Maureen Perry-Jenkins, Rena L. Repetti, and Ann C. Crouter, "Work and Family in the 1990s," *Journal of Marriage and Family* 62, no. 4 (2000): 981–998.
11. W. Cunningham and P. Villaseñor, "Employer voices, employer demands, and implications for public skills development policy connecting the labor and education sectors," *World Bank Research Observer* 31, no. 1 (2016): 102–134; E. A. Hanushek, G. Schwerdt, S. Wiederhold, and L. Woessmann, "Coping with change: International differences in the returns to skills," *Economics Letters* 153 (2017): 15–19; D. Krueger and K. B. Kumar, "Skill-specific rather than general education: A reason for US-Europe growth differences?" *Journal of Economic Growth* 9, no. 2 (2004): 167–207.
12. Thomas K. Maran, Simon Liegl, Andrés Davila, Sebastian Moder, Sascha Kraus, and Raj V. Mahto, "Who fits into the digital workplace? Mapping digital self-efficacy and agility onto psychological traits," *Technological Forecasting and Social Change* 175 (2022): 121352.
13. Jack Kelly, "How AI-Powered Tech Can Help Recruiters and Hiring Managers Find Candidates Quicker and More Efficiently," *Forbes*, March 15, 2023, https://www.forbes.com/sites/jackkelly/2023/03/15/how-ai-powered-tech-can-help-recruiters-and-hiring-managers-find-candidates-quicker-and-more-efficiently.
14. Rodney A. McCloy, Patrick J. Rottinghaus, Chan Jeong Park, Rich Feller, and Todd Bloom, "YouScience: Mitigating the skills gap by addressing the gender imbalance in high-demand careers," *Industrial and Organizational Psychology* 13, no. 3 (2020): 426–441.
15. Dr. Dhanurjay Patil, personal communication, August 21, 2022.

16. Matthew Mariani, "Replace with a database: O*Net replaces the Dictionary of Occupational Titles," *Occupational Outlook Quarterly* Spring (1999): 3–9, https://www.bls.gov/careeroutlook/1999/Spring/art01.pdf.

CHAPTER 2: READY, SET, GO!

1. McKenna Burrows, personal communication, July 11, 2021.
2. YouScience is the leading technology provider dedicated to solving the skills gap crisis for students and employers. Its end-to-end platform, YouScience Brightpath, connects education with career applications designed to help students unlock their potential for future pathways. YouScience leverages proven research, artificial intelligence, and industry input to help individuals identify their natural talents, validate their skills and knowledge, and get matched with real-world educational and career pathways in high-demand occupations. YouScience is the preferred choice of individuals, parents, educators, and counselors to guide and support educational and career pathways, currently serving more than seven thousand educational institutions and nearly one million users.

PART II: YOUR CORE FOUR

1. Howard I. Kushner, "Retaining the King's Left Hand," *The Lancet* 377, no. 9782 (2011): 1998–1999.
2. Lily Rothman, "How Lefties First Gained Acceptance," *Time*, August 13, 2015, https://time.com/3978951/lefties-history.
3. "The Left Hand of (Supposed) Darkness," *Merriam-Webster Dictionary*, https://www.merriam-webster.com/words-at-play/sinister-left-dexter-right-history.

CHAPTER 3: SPATIAL VISUALIZATION

1. Jan Ransom, "Here's What the Thanksgiving Parade Looked Like in Pandemic New York," *New York Times*, November 26, 2020, https://www.nytimes.com/2020/11/26/nyregion/thanksgiving-day-parade.html.
2. Galton is, deservedly, a controversial figure. Like many nineteenth-century investigators in what would ultimately become the modern study of human psychology, he was motivated by the perverse belief that certain races were superior to others, coining the term *eugenics* in his 1883 book, *Inquiries into Human Faculty and Its Development*. We deplore this idea.
3. Francis Galton, *Hereditary Genius: An Inquiry into Its Laws and Consequences* (London: MacMillan, 1869), 62, 140, https://galton.org/books/hereditary-genius/1869-FirstEdition/hereditarygenius1869galt.pdf.

4. Francis Galton, "Statistics of Mental Imagery," *Mind* 5, no. 19 (1880): 301–318.

5. "Aviation Cadet Training for the Army Air Forces" (United States Army, 1943), 1, https://history.cap.gov/files/original/e608b27f09bb897648ef5b7e3a348a95.pdf.

6. "Aviation Cadet Training for the Army Air Forces" (United States Army, 1943), https://history.cap.gov/files/original/e608b27f09bb897648ef5b7e3a348a95.pdf.

7. "A Report on the Purpose, Development and Validation of Test AC-10-A" (Psychological Division, Army Air Forces, 1942), 12.

8. Gregory Park, David Lubinski, and Camilla P. Benbow, "Recognizing Spatial Intelligence," *Scientific American*, November 2, 2010, https://www.scientificamerican.com/article/recognizing-spatial-intel.

9. Z. Hawes, H. Moriah Sokolowski, C. B. Ononye, and D. Ansari, "Neural underpinnings of numerical and spatial cognition: An fMRI meta-analysis of brain regions associated with symbolic number, arithmetic, and mental rotation," *Neuroscience & Biobehavioral Reviews* 103 (2019): 316–33, https://doi.org/10.1016/j.neubiorev.2019.05.007.

10. Nicole McGowan, personal communication, August 9, 2021.

11. McKenna is now dreaming of a career in real estate. The summer before her senior year, she found an internship with a local real estate agent and plans to take the real estate exam as soon as she turns eighteen.

12. Pseudonym used at the speaker's request.

13. Jonas Sorensen, personal communication, August 2, 2021.

14. Nadine Cipriani, personal communication, August 17, 2021.

15. Olivia Mason, personal communication, July 10, 2021.

16. Brianna Bullentini, personal communication, July 10, 2021.

17. Brianna Bullentini, personal communication, July 10, 2021.

18. Nicholas Lore, *The Pathfinder: How to Choose or Change Your Career for a Lifetime of Satisfaction and Success* (New York: Touchstone Books, 2011), 223.

CHAPTER 4: IDEA GENERATION

1. Pat Shea, personal communication, June 2022.

2. Ruth McEnery Stuart and Albert Bigelow Paine, *Gobolinks, or Shadow-Pictures for Young and Old* (New York: The Century Co., 1896), ix.

3. "What's behind the Rorschach inkblot test?" *BBC News*, July 25, 2012, https://www.bbc.com/news/magazine-18952667.

4. As noted by psychologist Ray Simpson, "the number of figures drawn within 15 min. is no index of a person's creative imagination" because it only measures "speed in production," not originality. Ray M. Simpson, "Creative Imagination," *American Journal of Psychology* 33, no. 2 (1922): 234–243.

5. Mark A. Runco, *Creativity: Theories and Themes: Research, Development, and Practice* (Amsterdam: Elsevier, 2014).

6. Neuroscientists have found that the key to this creative idea generation is the medial prefrontal cortex (mPFC), a part of the brain linked to decision-making, motivation, and putting plans into action. In freestyle rap, activity in the mPFC surges together with memory retrieval while stimulation drops in the brain region associated with self-conscious reflection and working memory (the dorsolateral prefrontal cortex). See Elizabeth Beam, "The Neuroscience of Linguistic Improvisation," *Harvard Science Review*, May 1, 2014, https://harvardsciencereview.org/2014/05/01/linguistic -improvisation.

7. Alex Osborn, *Applied Imagination: Principles and Procedures of Creative Thinking* (New York: Charles Scribner's Sons, 1953).

8. Carla Hall, personal communication, July 23, 2022.

9. Lonnie Johnson, another Brainstormer, started out as an engineer for the Air Force and NASA, where he helped design spacecraft that have flown to Mars, Jupiter, and Saturn. But even the boundless possibilities of interplanetary voyaging could not quench his thirst for Idea Generation. Johnson also invented the Super Soaker, one of America's favorite all-time water toys, and the Johnson Thermo-Electrochemical Converter, a type of heat-based engine that produces energy by compressing and expanding hydrogen gas. He holds over a hundred patents (with more than twenty more pending), including a wet diaper detector, a voice-activated compressed-air toy gun, a hair-drying curler apparatus, a solid state cryocooler, a flying disk, and a fishing lure. "Dr. Lonnie Johnson" and "Patents Held by Lonnie Johnson," Lonnie Johnson website, http://lonniejohnson.com.

10. Joel Savitt, personal communication, August 12, 2022.

11. Carla Hall, personal communication, July 23, 2022.

12. Philip Gerard, "The 1970s: Fatal Distraction," *Our State*, August 31, 2021, https:// www.ourstate.com/the-1970s-fatal-distraction.

13. Margaret Thomson Crichton, "From cockpit to operating theatre to drilling rig floor: five principles for improving safety using simulator-based exercises to enhance team cognition," *Cognition, Technology and Work* 19 (2017): 73–84.

14. Kate Murphy, "What Pilots Can Teach Hospitals About Patient Safety," *New York Times*, October 31, 2006, https://www.nytimes.com/2006/10/31/health/31safe.html.

15. Chris Peterson, personal communication, November 27, 2022.

16. Margaret Thomson Crichton, "From cockpit to operating theatre to drilling rig floor: five principles for improving safety using simulator-based exercises to enhance team cognition," *Cognition, Technology and Work* 19 (2017): 73–84.

17. Chris Eaton, personal communication, August 31, 2021.

18. Adam Grant, Tweet posted at 12:37 p.m., August 29, 2022 by @AdamMGrant, https://twitter.com/adammgrant/status/1564291077024120834.

19. Joshua Swift, "Coding Warmups," *DEV*, May 2, 2018, https://dev.to/joshuaswift/coding -warmups--44oc.

20. Albert Bigelow Paine, *Mark Twain, A Biography, 1835–1910* (Project Gutenberg eBook, 2006), https://www.gutenberg.org/files/2988/2988-h/2988-h.htm.

21. Elizabeth Beam, "The Neuroscience of Linguistic Improvisation," *Harvard Science Review*, May 1, 2014, https://harvardsciencereview.org/2014/05/01/linguistic-improvisation.

22. Jonas Sorensen, personal communication, August 2, 2021.

23. Guilbert Gates, "Listen to Bob Dylan's Many Influences," *New York Times*, October 15, 2016, https://www.nytimes.com/interactive/2016/10/14/arts/music/bob-dylan-influences-playlist-spotify.html.

24. Holly Fowler, personal communication, January 2, 2023.

25. Thomas H. Davenport and Nitin Mittal, "How Generative AI Is Changing Creative Work," *Harvard Business Review*, November 14, 2022, https://hbr.org/2022/11/how-generative-ai-is-changing-creative-work.

26. "Has AI reached the point where a software program can do better work than you?" *NPR Morning Edition*, December 16, 2022, https://www.npr.org/2022/12/16/1143330582/has-ai-reached-the-point-where-a-software-program-can-do-better-work-than-you.

27. Melody Brue, "Microsoft Introduces Generative AI Tools to Boost Creativity," *Forbes*, October 10, 2023, https://www.forbes.com/sites/moorinsights/2023/10/10/microsoft-introduces-generative-ai-tools-to-boost-creativity/?sh=160deb645469.

CHAPTER 5: INDUCTIVE REASONING

1. Anastasiya Lebedev, "The Man Who Saved the World Finally Recognized," *MosNews*, May 21, 2004, https://www.brightstarsound.com/world_hero/mosnews-com.html.

2. Dylan Matthews, "39 years ago today, one man saved us from world-ending nuclear war," *Vox*, September 26, 2022, https://www.vox.com/2018/9/26/17905796/nuclear-war-1983-stanislav-petrov-soviet-union.

3. Lebedev, "The Man Who Saved the World Finally Recognized."

4. Editors of Encyclopaedia Britannica, "Korean Air Lines flight 007," *Britannica*, https://www.britannica.com/event/Korean-Air-Lines-flight-007.

5. Lebedev, "The Man Who Saved the World Finally Recognized." Indeed, as so aptly noted by a crazy American general contemplating nuclear war in the 1964 satirical comedy *Dr. Strangelove*, only immediate launch of "an all-out and coordinated attack on all their airfields and missile bases" would give the United States "a damn good chance of catching them with their pants down!"

6. "Stanislav Petrov was declared to have died on September 18th," *Economist*, September 30, 2017, https://www.economist.com/obituary/2017/09/30/obituary-stanislav-petrov-was-declared-to-have-died-on-september-18th.

7. David Hoffman, "'I Had a Funny Feeling in My Gut,'" *Washington Post*, February 10, 1999, https://www.washingtonpost.com/wp-srv/inatl/longterm/coldwar/soviet10.htm.

8. Lebedev, "The Man Who Saved the World Finally Recognized."

9. Lebedev, "The Man Who Saved the World Finally Recognized."

10. Casa Wilson, Lisa Cook, Thomas Jensen, Brandi Manes, and Holly Wilhelm, *Choosing Intelligently: A Practical Guide to Using Your Aptitudes* (Johnson O'Connor Research Foundation, 2021), 35.

11. This exercise has a nonverbal format that provides a more objective, unbiased, and reliable measure for all test takers. The Inductive Reasoning test doesn't measure how many facts you know. Instead, it tests how you make decisions and arrive at a conclusion when you don't have all the information you need. By removing advanced vocabulary or familiarity with a particular cultural context, this test minimizes the impact of your personal background, language abilities, and previous education on your results.

12. Chris Karlsmose, personal communication, June 7, 2022.

13. Evan Heit, "Brain imaging, forward inference, and theories of reasoning," *Frontiers in Human Neuroscience* 8 (2015): Article 1056.

14. "The Power of Inductive Reasoning," *Daily Coach*, December 12, 2019, https://the dailycoach.substack.com/p/the-power-of-inductive-reasoning.

15. Yoshihisa Kobayashi and Tetsuya Mitsudomi, "Management of ground-glass opacities: should all pulmonary lesions with ground-glass opacity be surgically resected?" *Translational Lung Cancer Research* 2, no. 5 (2013): 354–363.

16. Michael Worobey, "Dissecting the early COVID-19 cases in Wuhan," *Science* 374, no. 6572 (2021): 1202–1204.

17. Nadine Cipriani, personal communication, August 17, 2021.

18. Olivia Mason, personal communication, July 10, 2021.

19. American Psychological Association, "Why people believe in conspiracy theories, with Karen Douglas, PhD," *Speaking of Psychology*, episode 124, https://www.apa.org/news/podcasts/speaking-of-psychology/conspiracy-theories.

20. Carrington Fox, "I Changed the Path of My Life and Had the Time of My Life Doing It," *Breaking Ground*, March 23, 2018, https://www.nccer.org/news-research/news room/blogpost/breaking-ground-the-nccer-blog/2018/03/23/i-changed-the-path-of-my-life-and-had-the-time-of-my-life-doing-it.

21. Carrington Fox, personal communication, July 11, 2021.

22. Carrington Fox, personal communication, July 11, 2021.

23. Xavier Russo, "Building an Organization with High Decision Velocity," *Medium*, August 8, 2021, https://medium.com/seek-blog/building-an-organization-with-high-decision-velocity-db9a29fde474.

24. Amazon Staff, "2016 Letter to Shareholders," Amazon, April 17, 2017, https://www.aboutamazon.com/news/company-news/2016-letter-to-shareholders.

25. Sarah Quessenberry, personal communication, June 15, 2022.

26. Sarah Quessenberry, personal communication, June 15, 2022.

27. "A Type of Reasoning AI Can't Replace," *Mind Matters*, October 10, 2019, https://mindmatters.ai/2019/10/a-type-of-reasoning-ai-cant-replace.

28. Adrian Bridgwater, "How Computer Brains Learn Human Reasoning," *Forbes*, June 15, 2016, https://www.forbes.com/sites/adrianbridgwater/2016/06/15/how-computer-brains-learn-human-reasoning/?sh=3fb3f25e13d4.

29. "A Type of Reasoning AI Can't Replace," *Mind Matters*.

CHAPTER 6: SEQUENTIAL REASONING

1. Catherine Stoddard, "Yeti coolers wash up on Alaska shores months after ship loses cargo," Fox 6, December 15, 2022, https://www.fox6now.com/news/yeti-coolers-wash-up-on-alaska-shores-months-after-ship-loses-cargo; and "Zim Kingston's Lost Cargo Included a Present for Beachcombers," *Maritime Executive*, December 5, 2022, https://maritime-executive.com/article/zim-kingston-s-lost-cargo-included-a-present-for-beachcombers.
2. These numbers may seem shocking, but they actually account for only 1 percent of the estimated 226 million shipping containers navigating the world's oceans. Ryan Stetson, "How many shipping containers are lost at sea annually?" Container Addict, https://www.containeraddict.com/how-many-shipping-containers-are-lost-at-sea.
3. Jonathan Franklin, "Ship carrying thousands of luxury cars sinks in the Atlantic after burning for weeks," *NPR*, March 1, 2022, https://www.npr.org/2022/03/01/1083790442/porsche-volkswagen-cargo-ship-sinks.
4. Ben Day, personal communication, July 26, 2021.
5. Samuel P. Horton, *Experiments with a New Form of Reasoning Test* (Boston: Human Engineering Laboratory, 1939).
6. D. J. Patil, personal communication, August 21, 2022.
7. Zach Leggett, personal communication, July 11, 2021.
8. John Hamm, "The Five Messages Leaders Must Manage," *The Harvard Business Review*, May 2006, https://hbr.org/2006/05/the-five-messages-leaders-must-manage.
9. Heather Holler, personal communication, July 27, 2022.
10. Zach Leggett, personal communication, July 11, 2021.
11. Mary Kenny, personal communication, January 3, 2023.
12. Marcus Wright, personal communication, May 26, 2022.
13. Charlie Plumb, "A Captain's Life," https://charlieplumb.com.
14. Kare Anderson, "Who Packs Your Parachute?" *Forbes*, November 18, 2015.

CHAPTER 7: VISUAL COMPARISON SPEED AND NUMERICAL REASONING

1. Stephenie Riley, personal communication, June 24, 2022.
2. "The £8.8m typo: How one mistake killed a family business," *Guardian*, January 28, 2015, https://www.theguardian.com/law/shortcuts/2015/jan/28/typo-how-one-mistake-killed-a-family-business-taylor-and-sons.
3. "Vatican pulls papal medal which misspelled name of Jesus," BBC, October 11, 2013, https://www.bbc.com/news/world-europe-24489512.
4. Fiona Simpson, "A rare copy of Harry Potter sold for £43,750 because of a spelling mistake," *Insider*, November 11, 2016, https://www.insider.com/copy-of-harry-potter-sells-for-43000-because-of-a-spelling-mistake-2016-11.

5. Nathan McAlone, "The true story behind Google's hilarious first name: BackRub," *Insider*, October 5, 2015, https://www.businessinsider.com/the-true-story-behind-googles-first-name-backrub-2015-10.

6. On Second Thought, "The Psychology of Typos," *Medium*, May 1, 2018, https://medium.com/@OnSecondThought_27622/the-psychology-of-typos-985d5a391853.

7. Judy Beaver, personal communication, February 14, 2023.

8. D. J. Patil, personal communication, August 21, 2022.

9. Personal communication, August 21, 2022.

10. Pseudonym used at the speaker's request.

11. Wayne D'Orio, "Tackling Math Anxiety," *U.S. News and World Report*, May 12, 2022, https://www.usnews.com/education/k12/articles/tackling-math-anxiety.

12. Brian Kennedy, Richard Fry, and Cary Funk, "6 Facts about America's STEM Workforce and Those Training for It," Pew Research Center, April 14, 2021, https://www.pewresearch.org/fact-tank/2021/04/14/6-facts-about-americas-stem-workforce-and-those-training-for-it.

13. Richard Johnson, "Looking for an Upgrade? These are the Best Jobs for 2022," Glassdoor, February 2, 2022, https://www.glassdoor.com/research/best-jobs-for-2022.

14. David Smith, "So you thought Sudoku came from the Land of the Rising Sun . . ." *Guardian*, May 14, 2005, https://www.theguardian.com/media/2005/may/15/pressandpublishing.usnews.

15. Helen Brooker, Keith A. Wenes, Clive Ballard, Adam Hampshire, Dag Aarsland, Zunera Khan, Rob Stenton, Maria Megalogeni, and Anne Corbett, "The relationship between the frequency of number-puzzle use and baseline cognitive function in a large online sample of adults aged 50 and over," *Geriatric Psychiatry* 34, no. 7 (2019): 932–940.

CHAPTER 8: CHERRIES ON TOP:
THE OTHER AMPLIFIERS

1. Naomi Blumberg, "Odyssey," *Encyclopaedia Britannica*, https://www.britannica.com/topic/Odyssey-epic-by-Homer.

2. Keith Hansley, "A Traditional Ancient Bard Would Need Around 50 Hours to Completely Sing Homer's Epics, the Iliad and the Odyssey," *Historian's Hut*, June 5, 2017, https://thehistorianshut.com/2017/06/05/a-traditional-ancient-bard-would-need-around-50-hours-to-completely-sing-homers-epics-the-iliad-and-the-odyssey.

3. Geoffrey S. Kirk, "Homer," *Encyclopaedia Britannica*, https://www.britannica.com/biography/Homer-Greek-poet.

4. Robert Kanigel, *Hearing Homer's Song: The Brief Life and Big Idea of Milman Parry* (New York: Knopf, 2021), 6, 103–105.

5. Arlin Cuncic, "What Is Associative Memory?" *Verywell Mind*, August 3, 2022, https://www.verywellmind.com/what-is-associative-memory-5198601.

6. Tessa Easley, personal communication, March 3, 2023.
7. Nate Smitherman, personal communication, April 14, 2022.
8. Sam Cade, personal communication, April 24, 2022.
9. Brooke Nelson, "15 Memory Exercises Proven to Keep Your Brain Sharp," *Healthy*, June 27, 2022, https://www.thehealthy.com/aging/mind-memory/memory-exercises.
10. John Grashel, "The Measurement of Musical Aptitude in 20th Century United States: A Brief History," *Bulletin of the Council for Research in Music Education* 176 (2008): 45–49; and Sheetal R. Modi, "Name That Tone! Test Your Tonal Recognition with Perfect Pitch," *Discover*, April 30, 2014, https://www.discovermagazine.com/mind/name-that-tone-test-your-tonal-recognition-with-perfect-pitch.
11. Chris Heckmann, "What Is Iambic Pentameter? Definition and Examples," StudioBinder, April 25, 2021, https://www.studiobinder.com/blog/what-is-iambic-pentameter-definition-literature/#:~:text=Iambic%20Pentameter%20Meaning&text=Think%20about%20it%20this%20way.
12. "Whistled Language of the Island of La Gomera (Canary Islands), the Silbo Gomero," UNESCO Video and Sound Collections, 2009, https://www.unesco.org/archives/multimedia/document-370.
13. Anna Wiener, "The Weird, Analog Delights of Foley Sound Effects," *New Yorker*, June 27, 2022, https://www.newyorker.com/magazine/2022/07/04/the-weird-analog-delights-of-foley-sound-effects.
14. Alix Spiegel and Elena Renken, "Her incredible sense of smell is helping scientists find new ways to diagnose disease," *NPR Invisibilia*, March 23, 2020, https://www.npr.org/sections/health-shots/2020/03/23/820274501/her-incredible-sense-of-smell-is-helping-scientists-find-new-ways-to-diagnose-di.

CHAPTER 9: WORK APPROACH AND INTERPERSONAL STYLE

1. Alexis Elcox, "100 Best Ted Lasso Quotes," Sarah Scoop, January 5, 2022, https://sarahscoop.com/100-best-ted-lasso-quotes.
2. Blair Downing, personal communication, June 22, 2022.
3. Marcus Wright, personal communication, May 26, 2022.
4. Olivia Mason, personal communication, July 10, 2021.
5. Brent Hull, personal communication, May 27, 2022.
6. Olivia Mason, personal communication, July 10, 2021.
7. Brent Hull, personal communication, May 27, 2022.
8. Jonas Sorensen, personal communication, August 2, 2021.
9. Blair Downing, personal communication, June 22, 2022.
10. Susan Cain, "Three Introverted CEOs and What You Can Learn From Them," *Quiet Revolution*, https://quietrev.com/3-introverted-ceos-and-what-you-can-learn-from-them.

CHAPTER 10: SETTING A COURSE

1. Meg Jay, *The Defining Decade* (New York: Value, 2016), xxxiii.

2. Heather Long, "The New Normal: 4 Job Changes by the Time You're 32," https://money.cnn.com/2016/04/12/news/economy/millennials-change-jobs-frequently/.

3. Rodney A. McCloy, Patrick J. Rottinghaus, Chan Jeong Park, Rich Feller, and Todd Bloom, "YouScience: Mitigating the skills gap by addressing the gender imbalance in high-demand careers," *Industrial and Organizational Psychology* 13, no. 3 (2020): 426–441.

4. Cambridge University Press, "YouScience: Mitigating the skills gap by addressing the gender imbalance in high-demand careers," November 11, 2020; and Alyson Klein, "Aptitude Tests: Are They Effective in Opening Students' Minds to More Career Paths?" *Education Week*, April 27, 2021.

5. Thomas Gilovich, Victoria Husted Medvec, and Kenneth Savistky, "The Spotlight Effect in Social Judgment: An Egocentric Bias in Estimates of the Salience of One's Own Actions and Appearance," *Journal of Personality and Social Psychology* 78, no. 2 (2000): 211–222, https://pdfs.semanticscholar.org/3d2a/1c99395124bf9372e1493f314f6990a78473.pdf.

6. Thomas Gilovich, Victoria H. Medvec, and Kenneth Savitsky, "The Spotlight Effect in Social Judgment: An Egocentric Bias in Estimates of the Salience of One's Own Actions and Appearance," *Journal of Personality and Social Psychology* 78, no. 2 (2000): 211–222.

7. Maya Ziegler, personal communication, July 1, 2021.

8. Stephenie Riley, personal communication, June 24, 2022.

9. Zach Leggett, personal communication, July 11, 2021.

10. Eric Karpinski and Becca Labbe Karpinski, "Sticky Situations: Feeling Obsolete and in the Way?" *Psychology Today*, October 28, 2021, https://www.psychologytoday.com/us/blog/putting-happiness-work/202110/sticky-work-situations-feeling-obsolete-and-in-the-way.

11. Carla Hall, personal communication, July 23, 2022.

12. Joel Savitt, personal communication, August 12, 2022.

13. Chris Karlsmose, personal communication, June 7, 2022.

14. Adam Grant, "The Perils of Following Your Career Passion," TED Talk, March 27, 2019, https://www.ted.com/talks/worklife_with_adam_grant_the_perils_of_following_your_career_passion/transcript.

15. Tracy Crowley, personal communication, May 1, 2023.

16. Nellie Davis, personal communication, May 2, 2022.

Index